DENTAL FLOSS FOR THE MiND

A COMPLETE PROGRAM FOR BOOSTING YOUR BRAIN POWER

Michel Noir, Ph.D., and Bernard Croisile, M.D., Ph.D.

McGraw·Hill

New York   Chicago   San Francisco   Lisbon   London   Madrid   Mexico City
Milan   New Delhi   San Juan   Seoul   Singapore   Sydney   Toronto

The McGraw·Hill Companies

Library of Congress Cataloging-in-Publication Data

Noir, Michel, 1944–
    Dental floss for the mind / Michel Noir, Bernard Croisile.
        p.   cm.
    Includes bibliographical references.
    ISBN 0-07-144776-8

    1. Intellect—Problems, exercises, etc. I. Croisile, Bernard. II. Title.

    BF431.3.N65 2005
    153'.076—dc22   2005041715

1 2 3 4 5 6 7 8 9 0   DOC/DOC   0 9 8 7 6 5

ISBN 0-07-144776-8

McGraw-Hill books are available at special quantity discounts to use as premiums and
sales promotions, or for use in corporate training programs. For more information, please
write to the Director of Special Sales, Professional Publishing, McGraw-Hill, Two Penn
Plaza, New York, NY 10121-2298. Or contact your local bookstore.

This book is printed on acid-free paper.

Contents

Foreword

When I was asked to write the foreword for *Dental Floss for the Mind,* I was thrilled. As a neuropsychiatrist for the past 20 years, I have developed a keen understanding of and a deep appreciation for the importance of maintaining a healthy brain. The book you are about to read provides a comprehensive, yet fun, exercise program that will boost your brain power and sharpen your cognitive skills.

Oscar Wilde once said, "The great sins of the world take place in the brain: but it is in the brain that everything takes place.... It is in the brain that the poppy is red, that the apple is odorous, that the skylark sings."

Fitting it is, then, that we acknowledge the need to devote more time to loving, nurturing, and feeding our brains. It seems these days that people spend more time, energy, and money on their "outer" beauty while devoting little or no time at all to their body's most important organ. There are pills to help us get skinny and surgeries to make us look like supermodels, but none of these efforts is going to make a difference if our most important organ isn't operating at an optimized level.

The brain is the most complex organ in the universe. There are more connections in the brain than there are stars in the universe, and studies have shown that while new learning causes new connections, not learning actually causes disconnections. By making new connections in the brain, we can delay and perhaps even prevent potentially serious, debilitating diseases such as dementia and Alzheimer's disease.

I encourage you to turn off the TV and work your brain. Work to learn something new every day. Einstein said that if you study anything for 15 minutes a day, in a year you will be an expert. Time to get back to the books and time to "floss." This is the book that will help you get your brain fit.

Daniel Amen, M.D.

Introduction

In *Dental Floss for the Mind,* you'll find a complete program designed to boost your brain power by stimulating five key cognitive functions: attention, memory, language, visual and spatial acuity, and reasoning. You use these functions in your daily life in a very casual but efficient way. However, numerous studies have shown that with regular practice and concentrated effort, you can improve the ease and speed with which these cognitive skills function, thereby boosting your brain's power and keeping this vital organ healthy and strong.[1]

Dental Floss for the Mind features 120 dynamic cognitive exercises at different skill levels. Studies have shown that improvement is more rapidly and easily achieved when mental exercise is playful and varied—hence the broad spectrum of exercises. Once you become familiar with an easy version of an exercise set, you will find it easier to solve the harder ones.

Thanks to these exercises, you will see your attention, memory, language, reasoning, and visual and spatial skills improve. It is then up to you to take advantage of this in your daily life. The exercises won't keep you from losing your car keys, but they will sharpen your cognitive skills so that you can find those missing keys faster than you ever have before.

What Are Cognitive Functions?

To be able to read and understand an article in the newspaper, to write a note with a pen, to recognize a colleague of yours at the movies, to recall the first and last name of your son's new friend, to make an arithmetic calculation, to have a discussion with your neighbor, to button your shirt, to know that a rose is a flower, to remember what your aunt's house looked like, to take the right road to work, to know

---

[1]Neubauer AC, Grabner RH, Freudenthaler HH, et al. Intelligence and individual differences in becoming neurally efficient. *Acta Psychol (Amst)* 116(1):55–74, May 2004.

Stevens B. How seniors learn. *Issue Brief Cent Medicare Educ* 4(9):1–8, 2003.

Stern RG, Mohs RC, Davidson M, et al. A longitudinal study of Alzheimer's disease: measurement, rate, and predictors of cognitive deterioration. *Am J Psychiatry* 151: 390–396, 1994.

Fabrigoule C. Do leisure activities protect against Alzheimer's disease? *Lancet Neurol* 1:11, 2002.

where you parked your car, to know that Washington, D.C. is the capital city of the United States, to know how to ride a bicycle—all of these daily activities require a fit brain. More precisely, they call upon higher brain processes known as cognitive functions.

The main cognitive functions are attention, memory, language, visual and spatial acuity, and reasoning. Even though we spend valuable time and money to maintain a healthy body—exercising, eating right, getting the proper amount of sleep—and even though studies have proved that mental stimulation improves cognitive functioning, we often neglect our most valuable organ: the brain.

What is good for the body is also good for the brain. A balanced diet is necessary for optimal brain functioning, since the brain needs glucose, vitamins, and unsaturated fatty acids. It's also important to exercise regularly. Although the brain represents only two percent of our body weight, it uses about 20 percent of all the oxygen we inhale; it is the most vascularized organ of the body. When we exercise, our blood circulates faster, sending more oxygen to all parts of the body, especially to the brain. Getting enough sleep enables us to learn and easily process the events of the day. Tobacco use, excessive alcohol use, or too much stress not only prevents our bodies from performing well, it also impairs the functioning of the brain. When we take care of our bodies by eating well, getting enough sleep and exercise, and avoiding harmful behavior patterns, we also take care of our brains.

However, when it comes to the brain, there's one factor we often neglect: mental stimulation. We humans are creatures of habit; we tend to engage in the same activities and behavior patterns. The familiarity of our daily routine is comforting, but routine activities are not very stimulating for the brain.

In fact, the brain "prefers" novelty and unexpected events. As humans, our cognitive functions thrive and improve when we're faced with new ideas, events, and challenges. When we mentally challenge ourselves on a regular basis, we can maintain good intellectual potential as well as reduce our risk for age-related long-term memory loss.

How Can We Maintain Our Cognitive Functions?

As we age, our ability to concentrate decreases, and we aren't able to execute standard mental operations as quickly as we did when we were younger. We may also have difficulty remembering recently acquired memories. Unfortunately, we tend to focus on these minor memory losses instead of concentrating on all the information that we do remember.

Cognitive aging is usually attributed to the progressive loss of neurons (the cells that conduct nerve impulses), but neuron loss is less important than it was thought to be a few years ago.[2] We're discovering that more important than the number of neurons is the intensity of their connections—intensity that can be strengthened through mental stimulation.

Recent scientific studies have shown that activities that require taking initiative and careful planning, like gardening and traveling, are associated with a decreased risk of developing Alzheimer's disease. Other studies have shown that it's better for the mind to engage in manual activities, such as do-it-yourself projects, painting, gardening, playing an instrument, and participating in sports, than it is to watch television, attend meetings, and listen passively to conversations.[3]

To maintain sharp cognitive skills, it is necessary to vary your intellectual activities on a regular basis, and the exercises in *Dental Floss for the Mind* can help you do just that!

Practical Advice

Here are some practical tips and commonsense recommendations that will help you acquire good habits for maintaining your cognitive capacities on a daily basis—without a lot of effort!

Practice the art of focusing

In order to remember something, it is often useful to focus on what is being done as memorization occurs. For example, if you read a text without focusing, it is very likely that you will not remember a word of it. Similarly, if you have just put your glasses in an unusual place without consciously thinking "I am putting my glasses on the kitchen

[2]Bertoni-Freddari C, Fattoretti P, Solazzi M, et al. Neuronal death versus synaptic pathology in Alzheimer's disease. *Ann N Y Acad Sci* 1010:635–638, Dec. 2003.

Peters A. The effects of normal aging on myelin and nerve fibers: a review. *J Neurocytol* 31(8–9):581–593, Sept.-Nov. 2002.

Toescu EC, Verkhratsky A. Neuronal ageing from an intraneuronal perspective: roles of endoplasmic reticulum and mitochondria. *Cell Calcium* 34(4–5):311–323, Oct.-Nov. 2003.

Albert M. Neuropsychological and neurophysiological changes in healthy adult humans across the age range. *Neurobiology of Aging* 14:623–625, 1993.

Brody HD. Organization of the cerebral cortex. III. A study of aging in the human cerebral cortex. *Journal of Comparative Neurology* 102:511–516, 1955.

[3]Fabrigoule C, Letenneur L, Dartigues JF, Zarrouk M, Commenges D, Barberger-Gateau P. Social and leisure activities and risk of dementia: a prospective longitudinal study. *J Am Geriatr Soc* 43:485–490, 1995.

table near the vase," the chances are good that you will not immediately find them when you look for them.

Motivation can also play a critical role in focusing. For example, you may read a book about the geography of Spain. Your memorization of the information will be much greater if you read the book because you are going to visit the country or if your son is moving there. The same principle applies to practice. If you read information about how to ride a horse—but never ride one—you will likely forget most of what you've read. If you ride horses, however, practice will imprint the information of the book in your brain.

Mentally repeat the information you want to memorize

Studies have shown that repeating information that you have just learned helps to ensure its transfer into long-term memory, where it is more likely to be remembered. Memory is strengthened by repetition.

Think about the information you want to memorize

Asking yourself questions about the information you want to memorize increases the probability that it will eventually be stored in long-term memory. It deepens your understanding of the information, which is the basis of memorization. For example, you have a better chance of remembering that eating fat is bad for the heart if you wonder "why is it bad for the heart?", and an even greater chance if someone gives you an explanation. A deeper understanding of information makes it logical and clear in your mind, as well as more likely to be committed to memory.

Sum up the information

Making a summary of the information you need to retain enables you to extract its essential elements without overloading your short-term memory with unimportant details.

Organize the information you want to learn

Classifying the information you want to learn is also a useful step in memorization, especially when you have to remember a large amount of information, like a long shopping list.

When you organize information into logical categories (for instance, vegetables and dairy products), the memorization process becomes easier. Instead of remembering individual words, you remember the names of categories, and what is in the categories themselves will be retrieved more easily. Instead of remembering seven or eight items, you remember two categories, in which there are three or four items each. For example, if you go shopping, rather than trying to remember to buy tomatoes, lettuce, toothpaste, cake mix, ice cream, soap, and beans, try to remember three vegetables, two desserts, and two bathroom items. Remembering the category will trigger retrieval of what is in that category.

To memorize a string of numbers—like a telephone or credit card number—it is helpful to divide the numbers into pairs or groups of four. You can then link them to birth dates or other significant historical events that are familiar to you and that you can easily retrieve.

Create acronyms

Mnemonic devices like acronyms help make the process of memorization easier. If you use them regularly, they become efficient tools. For example, in memorizing a list of words, you can make up an acronym from their first letters, so that each letter acts as a trigger for the retrieval of the words.

Turn routine tasks into rituals

In order not to lose your keys, glasses, or important letters, you should always put an object in the same place, and—even better—in a place that is related to its function. In the same way, in order not to forget daily tasks, like watering plants or taking medications, you should perform them at the same time each day and use external time "landmarks" as an aid. For instance, if you always water the plants after the postman delivers the mail, you have an external cue to help you remember to do it!

Use spatial and temporal landmarks when retrieving information

Making note of spatial and temporal landmarks during the learning process is highly beneficial in helping you retrieve information later. For instance, if you want to remember where you have parked your car, it is very helpful to make a specific note of something distinctive in the surroundings, like a fire hydrant or a lamppost. To remember an itinerary along city streets that you aren't familiar with, turn around at regular intervals to visualize the return route. In this way, you can memorize visual elements in both directions—and lessen your chances of becoming lost when you return along the same route.

Create associations

Creating associations relating several items will help you memorize them. To learn a list of words, for instance, you can build a sentence or phrase that associates several words in the list. You can also associate a word with a familiar location or with an object in that location. To remember a PIN number, for example, you can relate the number (or each digit thereof) to a birth date, the number of your street, your age, or other important number.

For optimal results, use these strategies while you work the exercises in this book. Soon, you'll find yourself applying them to everyday life!

How to Use This Book

You are probably reading this book because you want to improve your cognitive skills, benefit from an outstanding memory, and make sure your neurons are in top shape! While this can't be done overnight, working through the exercises in this book is a great way to start.

Dental Floss for the Mind is divided into five sections, each concentrating on a particular cognitive skill: attention, memory, language, visual and spatial acuity, and reasoning. Within each of these sections, there are four exercise sets, each of which is intended to work your brain in a different way and thereby improve your cognitive skills.

It is important to read the introduction to each set of exercises before working them. The introduction provides an orientation to the exercises, as well as instructions and strategies for completing them.

Each set has six exercises, ranging from easy to difficult. The first two exercises in the set are easy (indicated by a single ● in the page header), the next two are of medium difficulty (●●), and the last two are difficult (●●●).

Solutions to most exercises are either at the bottom of the page or on the next page. Solutions to some exercises are self-checking; these exercises require you to answer questions on the following page, then check your answers by referring to the exercise content on the previous page.

Some of the exercises are timed. For example, in the exercise set "Words, Where Are You?" (pages 81–94), you are allowed a certain number of seconds to memorize words and their locations in a grid; once the time is up, you turn the page and complete the exercise. In another exercise set, "Embroidery" (pages 115–21), the speed with which you work the exercise is taken into account in calculating the number of neuro-points you earn. It is more important to give correct answers than speedy ones, although timing will be a factor in any exercise that you don't complete because you have run out of time.

For timed exercises, you should have a timer available. One with an alarm is ideal, since it signals the end of a time period without your having to constantly consult a watch or clock. An inexpensive kitchen timer works well.

Dental Floss for the Mind also features three graded exercise courses. The assessment chart at the end of each exercise indicates the number of neuro-points you earned on the basis of your performance, and there is a scoring chart for each course at the end of the book. The graded courses are the following.

- WARM-UP. Use this program of simple exercises to begin improving your cognitive skills. Begin with the exercise on page 5; the scoring chart is on page 204.
- PRACTICE. Use this program of more-challenging exercises to hone the skills you developed in the WARM-UP. Begin with the exercise on page 7; the scoring chart is on page 206.
- CHALLENGE. Use this program for the ultimate in brain stimulation. Begin with the exercise on page 11; the scoring chart is on page 208.

Dental Floss for the Mind can be used in several different ways.

- You can work through the exercises sequentially from the beginning of the book to the end, progressing from easy to difficult in each set before moving to the next set.
- You can flip through the book, selecting and working exercises that strike you as interesting.
- You can work through all the easy (or medium-difficulty or difficult) exercises from beginning to end.
- You can work through the exercises in one section, concentrating on a particular cognitive skill, like attention or language.
- You can follow one of the book's graded courses: the WARM-UP, PRACTICE, or CHALLENGE level. This method enables you to track and score your progress.

Whichever method you use, be sure to read the introduction to an exercise set before attempting any of its exercises. The introduction provides orientation and often includes rules and tips for successful exercise completion.

We hope you enjoy the mental stimulation that *Dental Floss for the Mind* offers!

At one time or another you have probably had trouble focusing, or someone may have told you, "You're not concentrating hard enough!" Attention is a complex cognitive function that is crucial in human behavior; it is involved in all your daily activities. With attention, an external event (a sound, a picture, a smell) or an internal event (a thought, a memory) is selected by your mind and brought into consciousness.

Attention may occur in an automatic, passive fashion or in a voluntary, active fashion. If you hear a sudden noise, such as thunder, you automatically focus on it. This shift of attention is an automatic, involuntary reaction to a noteworthy event. Attention is highly sensitive to changes in your immediate environment. This quality, "alertness," enables you to be vigilant and to shift your attention quickly.

If you're walking along a busy city street and suddenly feel hungry, your attention may focus on your hunger, and that focus may help you to spot an open bakery. This voluntary shift of attention occurs when a personal, subjective event occurs, and it helps you achieve a specific goal. Voluntary shifts of attention also play an essential role in behavior.

Since it is impossible for your brain to simultaneously process all the sensory information available to it at any given moment, your brain successively analyzes the information. How does your mind determine which items in this flow of information take priority, and in what order? A cognitive mechanism called "selective attention" intervenes to select the most relevant information. This relevance is determined in accordance with your expectations and your situation. Selective attention works like a spotlight, highlighting relevant items while the rest remain in the dark.

The interaction between memory and attention is significant, since attention is activated only when something new has to be processed—something that is not already part of your memory. Indeed, when the information is known or familiar (like a painting that hangs in your living room), it does not draw your attention, and your brain processes its existence in an automatic fashion. There is no reason for your attention to be called to it, unless you notice something different about it (the painting is hanging crooked) or you have a particular reason to focus on it (you want to show it to your friends).

In daily life, your attention is constantly being called upon, as in situations where there are multiple tasks to perform and your attention must be divided among them. Unfortunately, as you age, you may notice a decrease in your attention resources, as well as a greater sensitivity to events that interfere with focusing.

Luckily, however, the exercises that follow will help you improve your attention skills. There are four sets of attention exercises.

- **Last Word**, in which you focus on each word in a sentence in order to arrive at the meaning of the text
- **Quick Fit**, in which you focus on the visual details of nearly identical images
- **Displaced Characters**, in which you practice sharpening your ability to observe
- **Odd One Out**, in which you focus your attention on a minute detail

Attention! Are you ready?

Last Word

This set of exercises will train your working memory while you engage in reading. Working memory helps you to temporarily keep certain items in mind while you are processing them. It involves processing what is read and heard, and it enables you to store words and meanings for a short period of time.

In this group of exercises, you will read sentences and try to memorize the last word of each sentence. You will record the remembered words on the following page, as well as answer a question about one of the sentences.

Carefully read the following four sentences and try to memorize the last word of each sentence. Then turn the page to continue the exercise.

Sibyl was seated comfortably enough in an easy chair, while Clare played the piano.

For a moment, the dancer spread her dark robe before her, like a wing.

By spring, the mother bear began leaving the cave on hunting expeditions.

The king had closed his eyes by this time and was dozing.

A *If you have read each sentence carefully, you should be able to answer the following question easily.*

What tone was the dancer's robe?

☐ deep

☐ black

☐ dark

B *Now write down the last word of each sentence in the same order as presented.*

_____

_____

_____

_____

WARM-UP

If your answer to A was ...	incorrect	incorrect	correct	correct
And you recalled this number of words correctly in B ...	0–3	4	0–3	4
Neuro-points earned	0	1	2	3

To continue your WARM-UP, turn to page 55.

Carefully read the following four sentences and try to memorize the last word of each sentence. Then turn the page to continue the exercise.

Bill and I had joint capital of about six hundred dollars.

The language arts teacher married his daughter to the history and geography teacher.

He was eating his sandwich hungrily, for he had eaten nothing since morning.

The bottles were kept cool in a canvas bucket that hung from the roof.

A *If you have read each sentence carefully, you should be able to answer the following question easily.*

How much was there in joint capital?

☐ six hundred dollars

☐ seven hundred dollars

☐ eight hundred dollars

B *Now write down the last word of each sentence in the same order as presented.*

_____

_____

_____

_____

If your answer to A was ...	incorrect	incorrect	correct	correct
And you recalled this number of words correctly in B ...	0–3	4	0–3	4
Neuro-points earned	0	1	2	3

To continue your PRACTICE, turn to page 63.

Carefully read the following five sentences and try to memorize the last word of each sentence. Then turn the page to continue the exercise.

A woman was watering roses in the garden of the first house to his right.

John and Miss March sat on her front step for a long time in silence.

He put his glass of red wine down and walked toward the staircase door.

The Yukon River was a mile wide and was hidden under three feet of ice.

Then he got matches out and proceeded to make a nice big fire.

A *If you have read each sentence carefully, you should be able to answer the following question easily.*

Where did John and Miss March sit?

☐ in the kitchen

☐ on the sofa

☐ on her front step

B *Now write down the last word of each sentence in the same order as presented.*

_____

_____

_____

_____

_____

WARM-UP

If your answer to A was ...	incorrect	incorrect	correct	correct
And you recalled this number of words correctly in B ...	0–3	4–5	0–4	5
Neuro-points earned	0	1	2	3

To continue your WARM-UP, turn to page 59.

Carefully read the following five sentences and try to memorize the last word of each sentence. Then turn the page to continue the exercise.

When he had finished, he filled his pipe and passed a leisurely time smoking.

The child was fully dressed and sitting on her father's lap near the kitchen table.

As my dad started the engine, I breathed on the window and, with my finger, I wrote my name.

In a few words, the commander explained the state of affairs.

While she spoke, she turned a silver bracelet round and round her wrist.

A *If you have read each sentence carefully, you should be able to answer the following question easily.*

Where was the child sitting?

☐ on her brother's lap

☐ on her father's lap

☐ on her sister's lap

B *Now write down the last word of each sentence in the same order as presented.*

_____

_____

_____

_____

_____

CHALLENGE

If your answer to A was ...	incorrect	incorrect	correct	correct
And you recalled this number of words correctly in B ...	0–3	4–5	0–4	5
Neuro-points earned	0	1	2	3

To continue your CHALLENGE, turn to page 65.

Carefully read the following six sentences and try to memorize the last word of each sentence. Then turn the page to continue the exercise.

I reminded my sister that I wished to go to the fair in the evening.

When Alicia came downstairs, she found Mr. Wild sitting by the fire.

The young lady observed me for a moment, then came over and asked me if I wished to buy anything.

A man stood on the railroad bridge, looking down at the swiftly flowing water below.

White as a ghost, Brian appeared at the entrance to the living room.

On Saturday nights, Rachel used to go to the movies with her friends.

A *If you have read each sentence carefully, you should be able to answer the following question easily.*

Brian was as white as ...

☐ a ghost

☐ an aspirin

☐ a skeleton

B *Now write down the last word of each sentence in the same order as presented.*

_____

_____

_____

_____

_____

_____

PRACTICE

If your answer to A was ...	incorrect	incorrect	correct	correct
And you recalled this number of words correctly in B ...	0–3	4–6	0–5	6
Neuro-points earned	0	1	2	3

To continue your PRACTICE, turn to page 57.

Carefully read the following six sentences and try to memorize the last word of each sentence. Then turn the page to continue the exercise.

This second passage of the moon was visible even to the naked eye.

It was nearly nine o'clock on a moonlit evening when a boat crossed the river with a single passenger.

He entered the tavern and was guided by the murmur of voices and the smell of tobacco.

She smiled and nodded to let me know that she was happy to be on that train.

She had gone to Rome to study art and produced a great many drawings there.

The journalist had written a very nice article about the dinner and the ensuing ball.

A *If you have read each sentence carefully, you should be able to answer the following question easily.*

Where had she gone to study art?

☐ Venice

☐ Paris

☐ Rome

B *Now write down the last word of each sentence in the same order as presented.*

_____

_____

_____

_____

_____

_____

CHALLENGE

If your answer to A was …	incorrect	incorrect	correct	correct
And you recalled this number of words correctly in B …	0–3	4–6	0–5	6
Neuro-points earned	0	1	2	3

To continue your CHALLENGE, turn to page 61.

Quick Fit

It is useful to be able to focus on a piece of information and to understand and memorize it. This is true not only with language and words, but also with shapes and figures.

This set of exercises will help you improve your ability to focus visually. You will analyze a set of shapes, paying attention to details, then extract those details moments later when you turn the page.

Look at the four figures below for 40 seconds. Then turn the page.

The four figures on page 19 are grouped below with similar figures. Find the four figures.

To help you, the order in which the figures are presented is the same as their order on page 19.

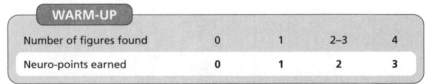

WARM-UP

Number of figures found	0	1	2–3	4
Neuro-points earned	0	1	2	3

To continue your WARM-UP, turn to page 69.

Look at the four figures below for 40 seconds. Then turn the page.

The four figures on page 21 are grouped below with similar figures. Find the four figures.

To help you, the order in which the figures are presented is the same as their order on page 21.

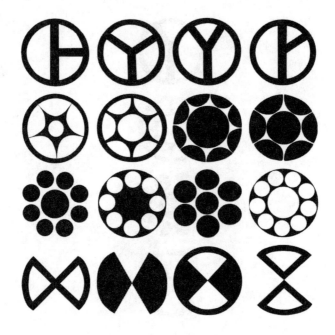

To continue your PRACTICE, turn to page 77.

Look at the four figures below for 40 seconds. Then turn the page.

The four figures on page 23 are grouped below with similar figures.
Find the four figures.

The figures may be anywhere in the group.

To continue your WARM-UP, turn to page 73.

WARM-UP

Number of figures found	0	1	2–3	4
Neuro-points earned	0	1	2	3

Look at the four figures below for 40 seconds. Then turn the page.

The four figures on page 25 are grouped below with similar figures. Find the four figures.

The figures may be anywhere in the group.

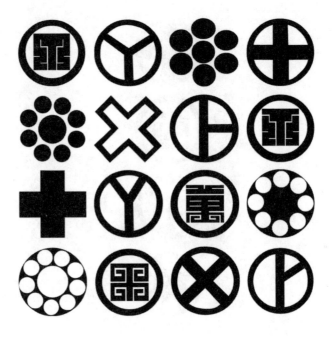

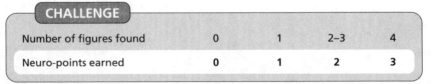

CHALLENGE

Number of figures found	0	1	2–3	4
Neuro-points earned	0	1	2	3

To continue your CHALLENGE, turn to page 79.

Look at the six figures below for one minute. Then turn the page.

The six figures on page 27 are grouped below with similar figures. Find the six figures.

The figures may be anywhere in the group.

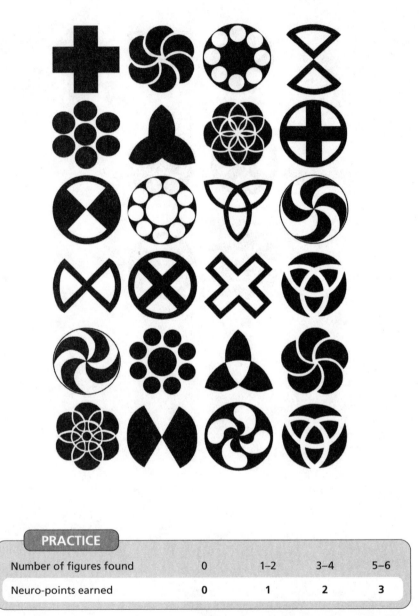

PRACTICE				
Number of figures found	0	1–2	3–4	5–6
Neuro-points earned	0	1	2	3

To continue your PRACTICE, turn to page 71.

Look at the six figures below for one minute. Then turn the page.

The six figures on page 29 are grouped below with similar figures. Find the six figures.

The figures may be anywhere in the group.

Number of figures found	0	1–2	3–4	5–6
Neuro-points earned	0	1	2	3

To continue your CHALLENGE, turn to page 75.

Displaced Characters

It is not always easy to understand a complex figure or plan at a single glance. To do so, you need strong visual focus, skillful analysis, and a sense of spatial movement.

This set of exercises will help you fine-tune these skills. Of the two groups of characters presented, the ones on the left are the reference group. You will examine them carefully, then select each character on the right that is not in the reference group on the left.

Keep in mind that the characters may have switched position.

In the image below, there are two sets of hieroglyphic characters. The group on the left is the reference group. Find every character on the right that is not in the reference group on the left. Try to do this in 30 seconds or less.

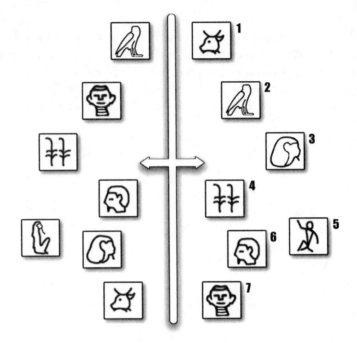

WARM-UP				
If you made this many mistakes ...	more than 1	1	0	0
And your time was ...	—	—	more than 30 seconds	less than 30 seconds
Neuro-points earned	0	1	2	3

To continue your WARM-UP, turn to page 83.

SOLUTION Picture 5 is not in the reference group.

In the image below, there are two sets of Thai characters. The group on the left is the reference group. Find every character on the right that is not in the reference group on the left. Try to do this in 30 seconds or less.

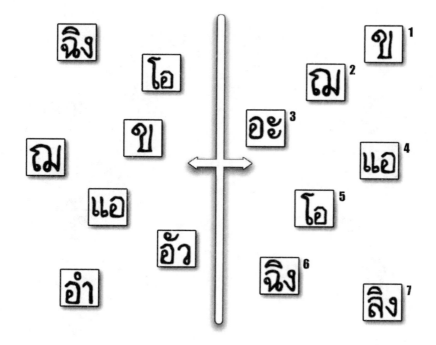

PRACTICE

If you made this many mistakes ...	more than 1	1	0	0
And your time was ...	—	—	more than 30 seconds	less than 30 seconds
Neuro-points earned	0	1	2	3

To continue your PRACTICE, turn to page 91.

SOLUTION Pictures 3 and 7 are not in the reference group.

In the image below, there are two sets of ancient Greek characters. The group on the left is the reference group. Find every character on the right that is not in the reference group on the left. Try to do this in 30 seconds or less.

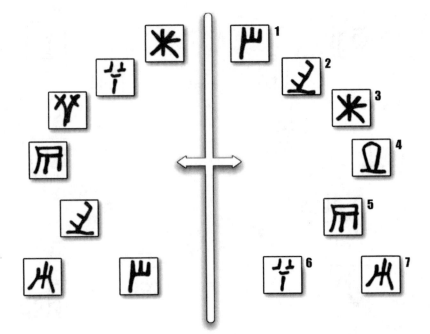

To continue your WARM-UP, turn to page 87.

WARM-UP				
If you made this many mistakes ...	more than 1	1	0	0
And your time was ...	—	—	more than 30 seconds	less than 30 seconds
Neuro-points earned	0	1	2	3

SOLUTION   Picture 4 is not in the reference group.

In the image below, there are two sets of Mayan characters. The group on the left is the reference group. Find every character on the right that is not in the reference group on the left. Try to do this in 30 seconds or less.

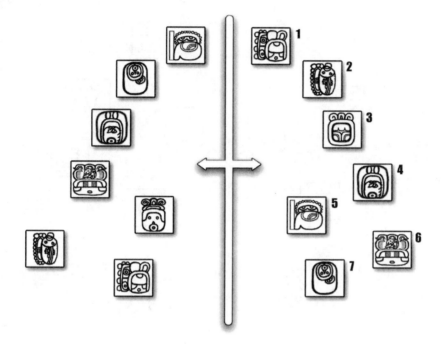

To continue your CHALLENGE, turn to page 93.

CHALLENGE

If you made this many mistakes ...	more than 1	1	0	0
And your time was ...	—	—	more than 30 seconds	less than 30 seconds
Neuro-points earned	0	1	2	3

SOLUTION *Picture 3 is not in the reference group.*

In the image below, there are two sets of Japanese characters. The group on the left is the reference group. Find every character on the right that is not in the reference group on the left. Try to do this in 30 seconds or less.

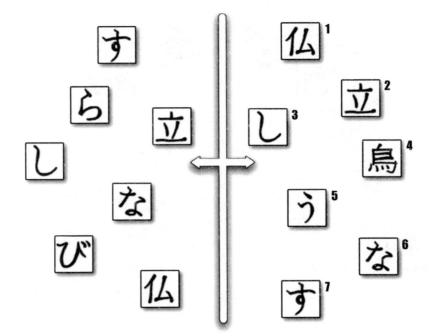

If you made this many mistakes ...	more than 1	1	0	0
And your time was ...	—	—	more than 30 seconds	less than 30 seconds
Neuro-points earned	0	1	2	3

To continue your PRACTICE, turn to page 85.

SOLUTION Pictures 4 and 5 are not in the reference group.

In the image below, there are two sets of Hindi characters. The group on the left is the reference group. Find every character on the right that is not in the reference group on the left. Try to do this in 30 seconds or less.

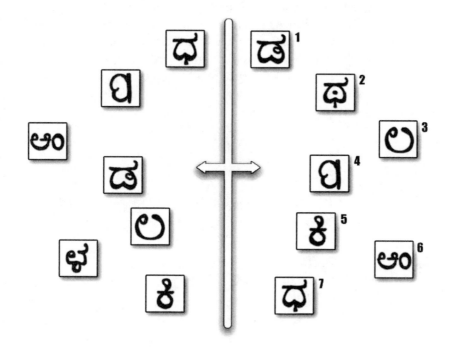

To continue your CHALLENGE, turn to page 89.

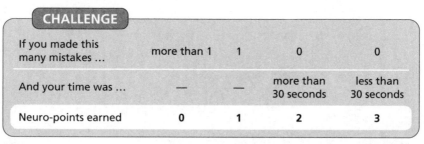

CHALLENGE

If you made this many mistakes ...	more than 1	1	0	0
And your time was ...	—	—	more than 30 seconds	less than 30 seconds
Neuro-points earned	0	1	2	3

SOLUTION Picturs 2 is not in the reference group.

Odd One Out

When you look at something, you visually detect a number of elements and determine their physical characteristics, such as color, shape, and orientation. The act of focusing allows you to make sense of these elements individually. In this way, you can find a needle in a haystack or, more realistically, a face in a crowd or an object in a room.

This set of exercises will train your visual exploration skills. A group of symbols is presented as a series; your objective is to find the odd one out as quickly as possible.

In one minute or less, find the odd symbols in the following series.

The odd symbol in this series: O

QQQQQQQQQQQQQQQQQQQQQQQQQQQQQQQQQQQQQQQQQQQQ
QQQQQQQQQQQQQQQQQQQQQQQQQQQQQQQQQQQQQQQQQQQQ
QQQQQQQQQQQQQQQQQQQQQQQQQQQQQQQQQQQQQQQQQQQQ
QQQQQQQQQQQQQQQQQQQQQQQQQQQQQQQQQQQQQQQQOQQQ
QQQQQQQQQQQQQQQQQQQQQQQQQQQQQQQQQQQQQQQQQQQQ
QQQQQQQQQQQQQQQQQQQQQQQQQQQQQQQQQQQQQQQQQQQQ

The odd symbol in this series: n

hhhhhhhhhhhhhhhhhhhhhhhhhhhhhhhhhhhhhhhhhhhhhhhhhhhhh
hhhhhhhhhhhhhhhhhhhhhhhhhhhhhhhhhhhhhhhhhhhhhhhhhhhhh
hhhhhhhhnhhhhhhhhhhhhhhhhhhhhhhhhhhhhhhhhhhhhhhhhhhhh
hhhhhhhhhhhhhhhhhhhhhhhhhhhhhhhhhhhhhhhhhhhhhhhhhhhhh
hhhhhhhhhhhhhhhhhhhhhhhhhhhhhhhhhhhhhhhhhhhhhhhhhhhhh
hhhhhhhhhhhhhhhhhhhhhhhhhhhhhhhhhhhhhhhhhhhhhhhhhhhhh

The odd symbol in this series: é

èèè
èè
èèèèèèèèèèèèèèèèèèèèèèèéèèèèèèèèèèèèèèèèèèèèèèèèèèèèèèèè
èè
èè
èè

The odd symbol in this series: P

RRRRRRRRRRRRRRRRRRRRRRRRRRRRRRRRRRRRRRRRRRRRRRRRRRRR
RRRRRRRRRRRRRRRRRRRRRRRRRRRRRRRRRRRRRRRRRRRRRRRRRRRR
RRRRRRRRRRRRRRRRRRRRRRRRRRRRRRRRRRRRRRRRRRRRRRRRRRRR
RRRRRRRRRRRRRRRRRRRRRRRRRRRRRRRRRRRRRRRRRRRRRRRRRRRR
RRRRRRRRRRRRRRRRRRRRRRRRRRRRRRRRRRRRRRRRRRRRRRRRRRRR
RRRPRRRRRRRRRRRRRRRRRRRRRRRRRRRRRRRRRRRRRRRRRRRRRRRR

Turn the page for the solutions.

SOLUTIONS *The empty circles below indicate the positions of the odd symbols in the series on the preceding page.*

QQQQQQQQQQQQQQQQQQQQQQQQQQQQQQQQQQQQQQQQQQQQQQQQQQQQQ
QQQQQQQQQQQQQQQQQQQQQQQQQQQQQQQQQQQQQQQQQQQQQQQQQQQQQ
QQQQQQQQQQQQQQQQQQQQQQQQQQQQQQQQQQQQQQQQQQQQQQQQQQQQQ
QQQQQQQQQQQQQQQQQQQQQQQQQQQQQQQQQQQQQQQQQQQQQQ(Q)QQQ
QQQQQQQQQQQQQQQQQQQQQQQQQQQQQQQQQQQQQQQQQQQQQQQQQQQQQ
QQQQQQQQQQQQQQQQQQQQQQQQQQQQQQQQQQQQQQQQQQQQQQQQQQQQQ

hhhhhhhhhhhhhhhhhhhhhhhhhhhhhhhhhhhhhhhhhhhhhhhhhhhhh
hhhhhhhhhhhhhhhhhhhhhhhhhhhhhhhhhhhhhhhhhhhhhhhhhhhhh
hhhhhhh(h h)hhhhhhhhhhhhhhhhhhhhhhhhhhhhhhhhhhhhhhhhhh
hhhhhhhhhhhhhhhhhhhhhhhhhhhhhhhhhhhhhhhhhhhhhhhhhhhhh
hhhhhhhhhhhhhhhhhhhhhhhhhhhhhhhhhhhhhhhhhhhhhhhhhhhhh
hhhhhhhhhhhhhhhhhhhhhhhhhhhhhhhhhhhhhhhhhhhhhhhhhhhhh

èèè
èèè
èèèèèèèèèèèèèèèèè(è è)èèèèèèèèèèèèèèèèèèèèèèèèèèèèèèèèè
èèè
èèè
èèè

RRRRRRRRRRRRRRRRRRRRRRRRRRRRRRRRRRRRRRRRRRRRRRRRRRRR
RRRRRRRRRRRRRRRRRRRRRRRRRRRRRRRRRRRRRRRRRRRRRRRRRRRR
RRRRRRRRRRRRRRRRRRRRRRRRRRRRRRRRRRRRRRRRRRRRRRRRRRRR
RRRRRRRRRRRRRRRRRRRRRRRRRRRRRRRRRRRRRRRRRRRRRRRRRRRR
RRRRRRRRRRRRRRRRRRRRRRRRRRRRRRRRRRRRRRRRRRRRRRRRRRRR
RR(R R)RRRRRRRRRRRRRRRRRRRRRRRRRRRRRRRRRRRRRRRRRRRRRR

WARM-UP

Number of odd symbols found	0	1–2	3	4
Neuro-points earned	0	1	2	3

To continue your WARM-UP, turn to page 96.

In one minute or less, find the odd symbols in the following series.

The odd symbol in this series: 🥟

The odd symbol in this series: ←

```
ﻉﻉﻉﻉﻉﻉﻉﻉﻉﻉﻉﻉﻉﻉﻉﻉﻉﻉﻉﻉﻉﻉﻉﻉﻉﻉﻉﻉﻉﻉﻉﻉﻉﻉﻉﻉﻉﻉﻉ
ﻉﻉﻉﻉﻉﻉﻉﻉﻉﻉﻉﻉﻉﻉﻉﻉﻉﻉﻉﻉﻉﻉﻉﻉﻉﻉﻉﻉﻉﻉﻉﻉﻉﻉﻉﻉﻉﻉﻉ
ﻉﻉﻉﻉﻉﻉﻉﻉﻉﻉﻉﻉﻉﻉﻉﻉﻉﻉﻉﻉﻉﻉﻉﻉﻉﻉﻉﻉﻉﻉﻉﻉﻉﻉﻉﻉﻉﻉﻉ
ﻉﻉﻉﻉﻉﻉﻉﻉﻉﻉﻉﻉﻉﻉﻉﻉﻉﻉﻉﻉﻉﻉﻉﻉﻉﻉﻉﻉﻉﻉﻉﻉﻉﻉﻉﻉﻉﻉﻉ
ﻉ←ﻉﻉﻉﻉﻉﻉﻉﻉﻉﻉﻉﻉﻉﻉﻉﻉﻉﻉﻉﻉﻉﻉﻉﻉﻉﻉﻉﻉﻉﻉﻉﻉﻉﻉﻉﻉﻉ
ﻉﻉﻉﻉﻉﻉﻉﻉﻉﻉﻉﻉﻉﻉﻉﻉﻉﻉﻉﻉﻉﻉﻉﻉﻉﻉﻉﻉﻉﻉﻉﻉﻉﻉﻉﻉﻉﻉﻉ
```

The odd symbol in this series: ♥

The odd symbol in this series: ⊻

```
♦ ♦ ♦ ♦ ♦ ♦ ♦ ♦ ♦ ♦ ♦ ♦ ♦ ♦ ♦ ♦ ♦ ♦ ♦ ♦ ♦ ♦ ♦ ♦ ♦ ♦ ♦ ♦
♦ ♦ ♦ ♦ ♦ ♦ ♦ ♦ ♦ ♦ ♦ ♦ ♦ ♦ ♦ ♦ ♦ ♦ ♦ ♦ ♦ ♦ ♦ ♦ ⊻ ♦
♦ ♦ ♦ ♦ ♦ ♦ ♦ ♦ ♦ ♦ ♦ ♦ ♦ ♦ ♦ ♦ ♦ ♦ ♦ ♦ ♦ ♦ ♦ ♦ ♦ ♦ ♦ ♦
♦ ♦ ♦ ♦ ♦ ♦ ♦ ♦ ♦ ♦ ♦ ♦ ♦ ♦ ♦ ♦ ♦ ♦ ♦ ♦ ♦ ♦ ♦ ♦ ♦ ♦ ♦ ♦
♦ ♦ ♦ ♦ ♦ ♦ ♦ ♦ ♦ ♦ ♦ ♦ ♦ ♦ ♦ ♦ ♦ ♦ ♦ ♦ ♦ ♦ ♦ ♦ ♦ ♦ ♦ ♦
♦ ♦ ♦ ♦ ♦ ♦ ♦ ♦ ♦ ♦ ♦ ♦ ♦ ♦ ♦ ♦ ♦ ♦ ♦ ♦ ♦ ♦ ♦ ♦ ♦ ♦ ♦ ♦
```

Turn the page for the solutions.

SOLUTIONS *The empty circles below indicate the positions of the odd symbols in the series on the preceding page.*

PRACTICE				
Number of odd symbols found	0	1–2	3	4
Neuro-points earned	0	1	2	3

To continue your PRACTICE, turn to page 100.

In 90 seconds or less, find the odd symbols in the following series.

Turn the page for the solutions.

SOLUTIONS *The empty circles below indicate the positions of the odd symbols in the series on the preceding page.*

WARM-UP				
Number of odd symbols found	0	1–2	3	4
Neuro-points earned	**0**	**1**	**2**	**3**

To continue your WARM-UP, turn to page 98.

In 90 seconds or less, find the odd symbols in the following series.

Turn the page for the solutions.

SOLUTIONS *The empty circles below indicate the positions of the odd symbols in the series on the preceding page.*

To continue your CHALLENGE, turn to page 101.

CHALLENGE

Number of odd symbols found	0	1–2	3	4
Neuro-points earned	0	1	2	3

In 90 seconds or less, find the unique symbols in the following series.

The unique symbol in this series:

The unique symbol in this series:

The unique symbol in this series: 1

PLTFIONGUCREFUQYWBFYZFEUYXZOUIAIOZWODZWEDIZCNTREYUSN8B
UEUORFORZUXUIUOEZQXPPQUZENCAMZ9RUCNANUC8EUR4NURZQ7ER
YCBZ7YQ32Q87P94VP32A45Q409VH6V09Z65C94Z9EZICQZIOR39CQ23N85
X7Q465BQ5X367B235V7N374NNVZ098BJTD09CZ34980Q9N78B2NB87BQVB
37518N54V6VQ540484V6B7VQ4MYBTFBLNWE4BYUVXQBTAEQTYVZW9EZR
YCNS9TUVTYNREXWURIROXQVITPEPSIRTCYEUBHUYNUUTFTCC65REZW

The unique symbol in this series: 8

7162534169304950764371614503969559403137465262354125496567459
65723156975426596354566974565472351523600552014590257036450123
0095674560325902108054630596574203210256300256965230147520123
0250236596547203021475021563096523014575421201236957659541230
0012355669657451526329212545710256340251204320569652305412705
96350621457095026300514775423695006956325417526395626541210074
59965369211235647005

SOLUTIONS *The empty circles below indicate the positions of the unique symbols in the series on the preceding page.*

PLTFIONGUCREFUQYWBFYZFEUYXZOUIAIOZWODZWEDIZCNTREYUSN8B
UEUORFORZUXUIUOEZQXPPQUZENCAMZ9RUCNANUC8EUR4NURZQ7ER
YCBZ7YQ32Q87P94VP32A45Q409VH6V09Z65C94Z9EZICQZIOR39CQ23N85
X7Q465BQ5X367B235V7N374NNVZ098BJTD09CZ34980Q9N78B2NB87BQVB
375 8N54V6VQ540484V6B7VQ4MYBTFBLNWE4BYUVXQBTAEQTYVZW9EZR
YCNS9TUVTYNREXWURIROXQVITPEPSIRTCYEUBHUYNUUTFTCC65REZW

716253416930495076437161450396955940313746526235412549656745965 72
315697542659635456697456547235152360055201459025703645012300956 74
560325902 0 054630596574203210256300256965230147520123025023659 65
472030214750215630965230145754212012369576595412300012355669657 45
15263292125457102563402512043205696523054127059635062145709502630
05147754236950069563254175263956265412100745996536921123564700525

To continue your PRACTICE, turn to page 97.

PRACTICE				
Number of unique symbols found	0	1–2	3	4
Neuro-points earned	0	1	2	3

In 90 seconds or less, find the unique symbols in the following series.

The unique symbol in this series: ?

%*<&~#{[ll'\^@@])="#&^)=]}<&~#{[ll'\^@@])=}{{@*"#&^)]}}{<&~#{[ll'\^@@]}
)={[<(_@)=]}}{{*"#)=]}}{{&^)<)=°+*&~@)=]}}{{*"#&^)<#{[ll'\^@@])=~!§>&"'(_-
)=°+*/-+.§!!!§://,<&~#{[ll'@)=]}}{{*"#&^)<@)=]}}{{*"#&^)<\^@@])=]}}{{[~!§(_-
)=°+*>&/,<&~#{[ll'\^@)=]}}{{*"#&^)<&~#{[ll'@)=,<&~#{[ll'@)=]}}]}}{{*"#&^)<@)
=]}}{{*"#&^)?<\^@@]})=&~#{[ll'\,<&~#{[ll'@)=]}}^@@])="#&^)=]}<&~#{[ll'\^@
@])=}{{@*"#&^)]}}{<&~#{[ll'\^@@])={[<(_@),<&~#{[ll'@)=]}}@)=]}}]}}{{*"#&^))

The unique symbol in this series: ↝

The unique symbol in this series: ♏

The unique symbol in this series: 🕐

Turn the page for the solutions.

SOLUTIONS *The empty circles below indicate the positions of the unique symbols in the series on the preceding page.*

%*<&~#{[ll`\^@@]})="#&^)=]}<&~#{[ll`\^@@]})=}{{@*"#&^)]}}{<&~#{[ll`\^@@]}
)={[<(_@)=]}}{{*"#)=]}}{{&^)<)=°+*&~@)=]}}{{*"#&^)<#{[ll`\^@@]})=~!§>&"'(_-
)=°+*/-+.§!!!§://,<&~#{[ll`@])=]}}{{*"#&^)<@)=]}}{{*"#&^)<\^@@])=]}}{{[~!§(_-
)=°+*>&/,<&~#{[ll`\^@])=]}}{{*"#&^)<&~#{[ll`@)=,<&~#{[ll`@)=]}}]}}{{*"#&^)<@)
=]}}{{*"#&^) <)^@@]})=&~#{[ll`\,<&~#{[ll`@)=]}}^@@]})="#&^)=]}<&~#{[ll`\^@
@])=}{{@*"#&^)]}}{<&~#{[ll`\^@@]})={[<(_@),<&~#{[ll`@)=]}}@)=]}}]}}{{*"#&^))

CHALLENGE

Number of unique symbols found	0	1–2	3	4
Neuro-points earned	0	1	2	3

To continue your CHALLENGE, turn to page 99.

MEMORY

Most of us forget important and not-so-important things on a regular basis: "I had completely forgotten today was George's birthday! Thank you so much for reminding me. Your memory is excellent!"

Memory is a crucial cognitive skill. With it, you remember your past experiences, as well as retain the knowledge you need for everyday tasks. We tend to see it as a whole, however, saying that we have "a good memory" or "a bad memory." In actuality, remembering what you ate yesterday uses a different part of the brain than remembering that Paris is the capital of France. Indeed, scientific studies show that different areas of the brain are activated according to what kind of information you are remembering. In fact, several groups of neurons in several areas of the brain can be simultaneously activated to build a memory.

Memory can be classified according to its duration and focus:

- *Sensory memory* is the most transient. It records new information perceived for just milliseconds.
- *Short-term memory* then takes over and stores the information for about one minute. When you read, your short-term memory is active, helping you remember the sentence you just read so that you can make sense of the next sentence.
- *Long-term memory* is used when you want to remember information for a longer period of time. This type of memory, which has unlimited content capacity and duration, contains all your long-lasting memories. Long-term memories can be stored for a long time and in several forms:
  - *Episodic memory:* When you recall something that you did yesterday, your last doctor's appointment, or a friend's birthday party, you are remembering personal events in context. This information is stored and retrieved by your episodic memory.
  - *Semantic memory:* Rules of grammar, the names of capital cities, and multiplication tables are general knowledge not linked to any particular memorization context; this type of information involves semantic memory. Although the information was initially of an episodic type (you first learned your multiplication tables in the context of Ms. Murray's classroom), it becomes semantic memory through abstraction of the spatial and temporal context in which it was memorized (you no longer think about Ms. Murray's classroom when you multiply 9 times 9). Semantic memory enables you to remember a fact without referencing the context in which you learned it.

- *Procedural memory:* The ability to automatically reproduce certain actions—playing the piano, riding a bicycle, or driving a car—involves your procedural memory. You perform these actions automatically, without conscious recall of the memory of learning the specific process.

Memory may be called upon and trained in multiple and varied ways. The four memory exercise sets that follow are a good starting point for improving your memory.

- **Tale Teller,** which helps you develop a method for understanding and memorizing texts
- **Complete Proverbs,** which brings cultural knowledge to mind by searching deep into memory
- **Words, Where Are You?,** which activates your visual and verbal memory capacities
- **Associations,** which reminds you of global semantic knowledge—and may even help you acquire and memorize knowledge in specific fields

Memory to the front!

Tale Teller

When you read, you recognize words that you know and can spell. But you also identify links between words and sentences. The sequence of links becomes meaningful when you organize what is read based on your own personal knowledge. This process is called comprehension. You organize what you read into a meaningful overview, as you interpret, adjust, and reinforce the meaning based on your previous knowledge.

As you read, you assign more importance to some words than to others, consciously or not—to verbs, for example, since they elaborate general ideas and structure the action.

In "Tale Teller," you will learn to understand a text by focusing on key words and establishing logical links between them. You will group verbs according to the order of their appearance. If you understand the text, it is easier to remember verbs in the proper order.

Read the following text carefully, then turn the page.

In a medium-sized town, two men lived in neighboring houses.

One day, one of the men developed such hatred of the other and envied him so much that the other man decided to find another home.

In that way, he hoped that his enemy would forget all about him.

So he sold his house and the little furniture it contained.

He moved to the capital of the country.

Write the verbs below in the order in which they appeared in the text on the preceding page.

1 _____3_____   decided

2 _____6_____   hoped

3 _____1_____   lived

4 _____~~4~~ 5_____   moved

5 _____2_____   developed

6 _____4_____   sold

To continue your WARM-UP, turn to page 107.

SOLUTION   1 lived 2 developed 3 decided 4 hoped 5 sold 6 moved

Read the following text carefully, then turn the page.

Mr. Sorrow gave me a look that was as hard as a blow between the eyes.

He had turned rather red,

got up from the comfortable red velvet armchair,

gathered his hat and gloves from the chair across the room,

and went out of the room, more furious than I'd ever seen him.

I remained there, speechless, long after dark.

Write the verbs below in the order in which they appeared in the text on the preceding page.

1 _____   gathered

2 _____   got up

3 _____   gave

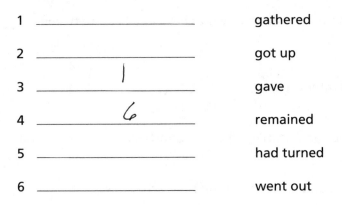

4 _____   remained

5 _____   had turned

6 _____   went out

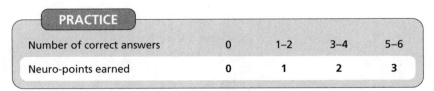

PRACTICE				
Number of correct answers	0	1–2	3–4	5–6
Neuro-points earned	0	1	2	3

To continue your PRACTICE, turn to page 111.

SOLUTION   1 gave 2 had turned 3 got up 4 gathered 5 went out 6 remained

Read the following text carefully, then turn the page.

They were heading straight toward the solid rock, which must have been well over a hundred feet tall.

When they were within fifty yards of it, Beryl finally saw their destination.

Through a break in the cliff, the yacht entered and very slowly traversed a narrow channel of crystal clear water between high gray walls.

Then they were riding in a miniature world of green and gold, a gilded bay smooth as glass and set about with tiny palms.

After passing through a farther rim of tropical vegetation, they came out on a pearl-gray virgin beach, where Beryl kicked off her brown golf shoes.

Write the verbs below in the order in which they appeared in the text on the preceding page.

1 _____   entered

2 _____   traversed

3 _____   saw

4 _____   kicked off

5 _____   were riding

6 _____   came out

7 _____   were heading

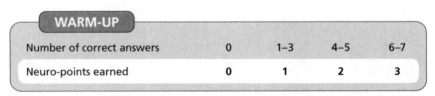

WARM-UP

Number of correct answers	0	1–3	4–5	6–7
Neuro-points earned	0	1	2	3

To continue your WARM-UP, turn to page 109.

SOLUTION   1 were heading 2 saw 3 entered 4 traversed 5 were riding 6 came out 7 kicked off

Read the following text carefully, then turn the page.

There was a sound—a warning. The aunts glanced up, trembling with fear.

There stood the doctor, his face a thundercloud.

Mother and child knew nothing of his presence.

The physician looked sullenly at the scene before him.

He studied it, searching for its genesis.

Then he put up his hand as a sign to the aunts.

They came trembling toward him and stood humbly before him, waiting.

He bent down, slowly and noiselessly, toward the three ladies.

Write the verbs below in the order in which they appeared in the text on the preceding page.

1 _____   knew

2 _____   put up

3 _____   glanced up

4 _____   came

5 _____   studied

6 _____   looked

7 _____   bent down

To continue your CHALLENGE, turn to page 113.

SOLUTION   1 glanced up 2 knew 3 looked 4 studied
5 put up 6 came 7 bent down

Read the following text carefully, then turn the page.

Nasby and I saw the machine through a window and went in
to look at it.

The salesperson showed us samples of its output and said
it could do 57 words a minute—

a statement that we frankly confessed we did not believe.

So he put his secretary to work, and we timed her.

She actually typed the 57 words in 60 seconds. We were partly
convinced, but said it probably couldn't happen again.

We timed the girl again and again—with the same result:
She won.

The price of the machine was one hundred twenty-five dollars.
I bought one, and we went away very excited.

Write the verbs below in the order in which they appeared in the text on the preceding page.

1 _____   went away

2 _____   saw

3 _____   bought

4 _____   won

5 _____   went in

6 _____   confessed

7 _____   timed

8 _____   put

9 _____   showed

10 _____   said

PRACTICE				
Number of correct answers	0	1–4	5–7	8–10
Neuro-points earned	0	1	2	3

To continue your PRACTICE, turn to page 108.

SOLUTION   1 saw 2 went in 3 showed 4 said 5 confessed 6 put 7 timed 8 won 9 bought 10 went away

Read the following text carefully, then turn the page.

The fresh morning air had caused the doctor to forget his troubles, and he came back about midday in excellent humor.

As he opened the hall door, the vile smell of chemicals greeted him harshly.

He entered the dining room and stood aghast at the sight.

Ida was sitting among her bottles, with a lit cigarette in her left hand and a glass of stout on the table beside her.

Clara, also holding a cigarette, was lounging in the easy chair with several maps spread out on the floor around her.

The doctor gazed from one to the other through the haze of smoke, but his eyes finally rested ruefully on his elder, more serious daughter.

Write the verbs below in the order in which they appeared in the text on the preceding page.

1 _____ came back

2 _____ stood

3 _____ gazed

4 _____ had caused

5 _____ was sitting

6 _____ was lounging

7 _____ opened

8 _____ entered

9 _____ rested

10 _____ greeted

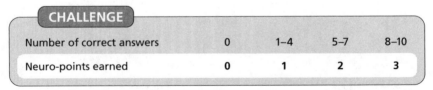

CHALLENGE

Number of correct answers	0	1–4	5–7	8–10
Neuro-points earned	0	1	2	3

To continue your CHALLENGE, turn to page 110.

SOLUTION 1 had caused 2 came back 3 opened 4 greeted 5 entered 6 stood 7 was sitting 8 was lounging 9 gazed 10 rested

Complete Proverbs

In the following exercises, you will put your cultural knowledge to the test. Read each incomplete proverb and supply the missing word(s). An answer is considered correct if it has the same meaning as the solution given, even if it differs by one or more words.

Supply the beginning words of each of the following proverbs.

1 _____ to tango.

2 _____ killed the cat.

3 _____ the doctor away.

4 _____ is another man's gain.

5 _____ louder than words.

6 _____ losers weepers.

7 _____ is golden.

8 _____ is human.

9 _____ those who help themselves.

10 _____ saves nine.

11 _____ is believing.

12 _____ the mother of all wisdom.

13 _____ like son.

14 _____ to godliness.

15 _____ the heart is.

Turn the page for the solutions.

SOLUTIONS

1 **It takes two** to tango.

2 **Curiosity** killed the cat.

3 **An apple a day keeps** the doctor away.

4 **One man's loss** is another man's gain.

5 **Actions speak** louder than words.

6 **Finders keepers,** losers weepers.

7 **Silence** is golden.

8 **To err** is human.

9 **God helps** those who help themselves.

10 **A stitch in time** saves nine.

11 **Seeing** is believing.

12 **Experience is** the mother of all wisdom.

13 **Like father,** like son.

14 **Cleanliness is next** to godliness.

15 **Home is where** the heart is.

WARM-UP

Number of correct answers	0	1–6	7–11	12–15
Neuro-points earned	0	1	2	3

To continue your WARM-UP, turn to page 116.

Supply the beginning words of each of the following proverbs.

1 _____ its weakest link.

2 _____ are soon parted.

3 _____ make light work.

4 _____ only skin deep.

5 _____ can't be choosers.

6 _____ the mice will play.

7 _____ before they are hatched.

8 _____ what you sow.

9 _____ with fire.

10 _____ than done.

11 _____ is his own worst enemy.

12 _____ to those who wait.

13 _____ and he'll take a yard.

14 _____ where credit is due.

15 _____ thicker than water.

Turn the page for the solutions.

SOLUTIONS

1 **A chain is no stronger than** its weakest link.

2 **A fool and his money** are soon parted.

3 **Many hands** make light work.

4 **Beauty is** only skin deep.

5 **Beggars** can't be choosers.

6 **When the cat's away,** the mice will play.

7 **Don't count your chickens** before they are hatched.

8 **You reap** what you sow.

9 **Fight fire** with fire.

10 **Easier said** than done.

11 **Every man** is his own worst enemy.

12 **All good things come** to those who wait.

13 **Give him an inch,** and he'll take a yard.

14 **Give credit** where credit is due.

15 **Blood is** thicker than water.

PRACTICE

Number of correct answers	0	1–6	7–11	12–15
Neuro-points earned	0	1	2	3

To continue your PRACTICE, turn to page 120.

Supply the beginning words of each of the following proverbs.

1 _____ than never.

2 _____ is bliss.

3 _____ catches the worm.

4 _____ number one.

5 _____ grow fonder.

6 _____ with pleasure.

7 _____ are better than one.

8 _____ is the spice of life.

9 _____ to pay Paul.

10 _____ goes unpunished.

11 _____ there's a way.

12 _____ the best medicine.

13 _____ a bowl of cherries.

14 _____ beware.

15 _____ no gain.

Turn the page for the solutions.

SOLUTIONS

1 **Better late** than never.

2 **Ignorance** is bliss.

3 **The early bird** catches the worm.

4 **Watch out for** number one.

5 **Absence/Distance makes the heart** grow fonder.

6 **Don't mix business** with pleasure.

7 **Two heads** are better than one.

8 **Variety** is the spice of life.

9 **Don't rob Peter** to pay Paul.

10 **No good deed** goes unpunished.

11 **Where there's a will**, there's a way.

12 **Laughter is** the best medicine.

13 **Life is just** a bowl of cherries.

14 **Let the buyer** beware.

15 **No pain**, no gain.

WARM-UP				
Number of correct answers	0	1–6	7–11	12–15
Neuro-points earned	0	1	2	3

To continue your WARM-UP, turn to page 118.

Supply the beginning words of each of the following proverbs.

1 _____ and eat it too.

2 _____ divided we fall.

3 _____ say never.

4 _____ deserves another.

5 _____ spoil the broth.

6 _____ the kettle black.

7 _____ all wounds.

8 _____ better than nothing.

9 _____ twice in the same place.

10 _____ May flowers.

11 _____ to every story.

12 _____ are free.

13 _____ justifies the means.

14 _____ is the hardest.

15 _____ another day.

Turn the page for the solutions.

SOLUTIONS

1 **You can't have your cake** and eat it too.

2 **United we stand,** divided we fall.

3 **Never** say never.

4 **One good turn** deserves another.

5 **Too many cooks** spoil the broth.

6 **That's like the pot calling** the kettle black.

7 **Time heals** all wounds.

8 **Something is** better than nothing.

9 **Lightning never strikes** twice in the same place.

10 **April showers bring** May flowers.

11 **There are two sides** to every story.

12 **The best things in life** are free.

13 **The end** justifies the means.

14 **The first step** is the hardest.

15 **Tomorrow is** another day.

CHALLENGE

Number of correct answers	0	1–6	7–11	12–15
Neuro-points earned	0	1	2	3

To continue your CHALLENGE, turn to page 121.

Supply the beginning words of each of the following proverbs.

1 _____ easy go.

2 _____ that feeds you.

3 _____ your own canoe.

4 _____ of my enemy is my friend.

5 _____ but it pours.

6 _____ far from the tree.

7 _____ soul of wit.

8 _____ in the mouth.

9 _____ breeds contempt.

10 _____ has a silver lining.

11 _____ over spilled milk.

12 _____ make good neighbors.

13 _____ to know one.

14 _____ it's worth doing well.

15 _____ twice shy.

Turn the page for the solutions.

SOLUTIONS

1 **Easy come,** easy go.

2 **Don't bite the hand** that feeds you.

3 **Paddle** your own canoe.

4 **The enemy** of my enemy is my friend.

5 **It never rains** but it pours.

6 **The apple doesn't fall** far from the tree.

7 **Brevity is the** soul of wit.

8 **Never look a gift horse** in the mouth.

9 **Familiarity** breeds contempt.

10 **Every cloud** has a silver lining.

11 **Don't cry** over spilled milk.

12 **Good fences** make good neighbors.

13 **It takes one** to know one.

14 **If a job's worth doing,** it's worth doing well.

15 **Once bitten,** twice shy.

PRACTICE				
Number of correct answers	0	1–6	7–11	12–15
Neuro-points earned	0	1	2	3

To continue your PRACTICE, turn to page 117.

Supply the beginning words of each of the following proverbs.

1 _____ will be boys.

2 _____ travels fast.

3 _____ rules the world.

4 _____ by its cover.

5 _____ in one basket.

6 _____ like an old fool.

7 _____ doesn't buy happiness.

8 _____ makes waste.

9 _____ gathers no moss.

10 _____ for the trees.

11 _____ garbage out.

12 _____ is the better part of valor.

13 _____ and be merry.

14 _____ to spite your face.

15 _____ feed a cold.

Turn the page for the solutions.

SOLUTIONS

1 **Boys** will be boys.

2 **Bad news** travels fast.

3 **The hand that rocks the cradle** rules the world.

4 **You can't judge a book** by its cover.

5 **Don't put all your eggs** in one basket.

6 **There's no fool** like an old fool.

7 **Money** doesn't buy happiness.

8 **Haste** makes waste.

9 **A rolling stone** gathers no moss.

10 **You can't see the forest** for the trees.

11 **Garbage in**, garbage out.

12 **Discretion** is the better part of valor.

13 **Eat, drink**, and be merry.

14 **Don't cut off your nose** to spite your face.

15 **Starve a fever**, feed a cold.

CHALLENGE

Number of correct answers	0	1–6	7–11	12–15
Neuro-points earned	0	1	2	3

To continue your CHALLENGE, turn to page 119.

Words, Where Are You?

Memory works through associations of ideas and pictures that enable logical organizations. In the following exercises, you'll practice memorizing words in specific locations in a grid. To do this, create links by first memorizing a word, then memorizing its location in the grid.

Throughout the exercises, you may want to create mnemonics—small hints or aids for memorization. For instance, if you see the word *cat* above the word *table* in a grid, you may remember the two words better if you think *The cat sits on the table.* You will soon find that linking language elements with visual ones makes the memorization process easier.

Allow yourself 30 seconds to memorize the six words and the location of each word in the grid below. Then turn the page.

umbrella				
		camera		mountain
				hedgehog
		bottle		
	needle			

Write each of the six words from the preceding page in the correct shaded rectangle below.

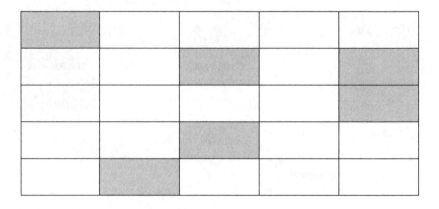

WARM-UP

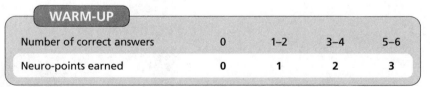

Number of correct answers	0	1–2	3–4	5–6
Neuro-points earned	0	1	2	3

To continue your WARM-UP, turn to page 123.

Allow yourself 30 seconds to memorize the six words and the location of each word in the grid below. Then turn the page.

	pencil		sympathy	
				rodeo
	car			
sugar			orange	

*Write each of the six words from the preceding page in the correct
shaded rectangle below.*

	Pencil			
				roll
	Car			
sugar			*orange*	

Allow yourself 45 seconds to memorize the eight words and the location of each word in the grid below. Then turn the page.

coat				
	square	dancer		
disease				tulip
			poem	
sun		armchair		

Write each of the eight words from the preceding page in the correct shaded rectangle below.

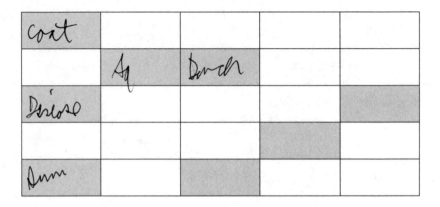

To continue your WARM-UP, turn to page 125.

Allow yourself 45 seconds to memorize the eight words and the location of each word in the grid below. Then turn the page.

		catalog		
horror				goddess
	fall		castle	
			window	
program		piano		

Write each of the eight words from the preceding page in the correct gray rectangle below.

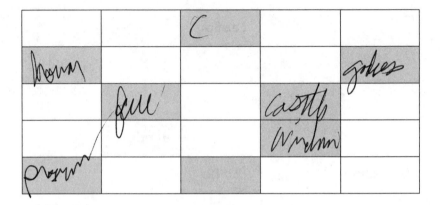

CHALLENGE

Number of correct answers	0	1–3	4–6	7–8
Neuro-points earned	0	1	2	3

To continue your CHALLENGE, turn to page 128.

Allow yourself 45 seconds to memorize the eight words and the location of each word in the grid below. Then turn the page.

	fan		travel	
			treason	
		apple		
hospital				eyebrow
		boat	cabin	

Write each of the eight words from the preceding page in the correct rectangle below. You have reached the difficult level, so rectangles are no longer shaded.

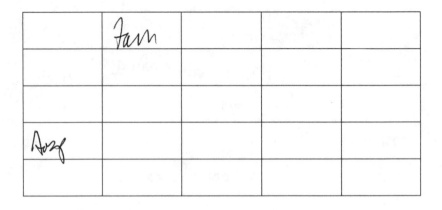

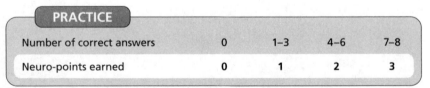

PRACTICE

Number of correct answers	0	1–3	4–6	7–8
Neuro-points earned	0	1	2	3

To continue your PRACTICE, turn to page 124.

Allow yourself 45 seconds to memorize the eight words and the location of each word in the grid below. Then turn the page.

	book			
			diamond	
silence		cherry		sadness
			violin	
	remains			feather

Write each of the eight words from the preceding page in the correct rectangle below. You have reached the difficult level, so rectangles are no longer shaded.

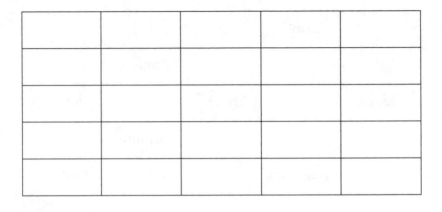

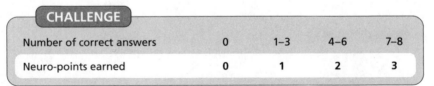

CHALLENGE

Number of correct answers	0	1–3	4–6	7–8
Neuro-points earned	0	1	2	3

To continue your CHALLENGE, turn to page 126.

Associations

Semantic memory comprises all your knowledge about general things in the world, from actual facts (geography and history) to public events (news and entertainment) to language (spelling and vocabulary). In the following exercises, you'll draw on this semantic memory to make associations. Don't worry if you aren't familiar with some of the terms in these exercises; this may help you identify further areas for study.

Match the terms in the first column with those in the second.

A *Match each actor with the movie in which he or she starred.*

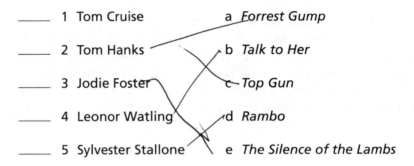

_____ 1 Tom Cruise   a *Forrest Gump*

_____ 2 Tom Hanks   b *Talk to Her*

_____ 3 Jodie Foster   c *Top Gun*

_____ 4 Leonor Watling   d *Rambo*

_____ 5 Sylvester Stallone   e *The Silence of the Lambs*

B *Match each state with its capital city.*

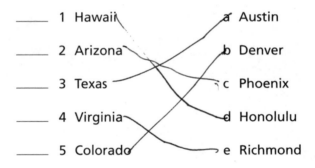

_____ 1 Hawaii   a Austin

_____ 2 Arizona   b Denver

_____ 3 Texas   c Phoenix

_____ 4 Virginia   d Honolulu

_____ 5 Colorado   e Richmond

WARM-UP				
Number of correct answers	0–4	5–6	7–8	9–10
Neuro-points earned	0	1	2	3

To continue your WARM-UP, turn to page 130.

SOLUTIONS A 1c 2a 3e 4b 5d B 1d 2c 3a 4e 5b

Match the terms in the first column with those in the second.

A *Match each animal with the animal group to which it belongs.*

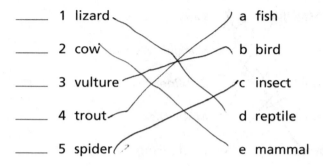

____ 1 lizard   a fish

____ 2 cow   b bird

____ 3 vulture   c insect

____ 4 trout   d reptile

____ 5 spider   e mammal

B *Match each monument with the city in which it is located.*

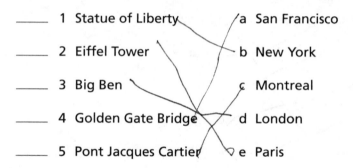

____ 1 Statue of Liberty   a San Francisco

____ 2 Eiffel Tower   b New York

____ 3 Big Ben   c Montreal

____ 4 Golden Gate Bridge   d London

____ 5 Pont Jacques Cartier   e Paris

PRACTICE

Number of correct answers	0–4	5–6	7–8	9–10
Neuro-points earned	0	1	2	3

To continue your PRACTICE, turn to page 134.

SOLUTIONS   B 1b 2e 3d 4a 5c
                 A 1d 2e 3b 4a 5c

Match the terms in the first column with those in the second.

A *Match each author with the book that he or she wrote.*

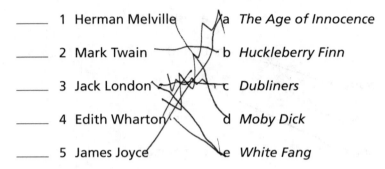

_____ 1 Herman Melville   a *The Age of Innocence*

_____ 2 Mark Twain   b *Huckleberry Finn*

_____ 3 Jack London   c *Dubliners*

_____ 4 Edith Wharton   d *Moby Dick*

_____ 5 James Joyce   e *White Fang*

B *Match each color tint with its closest basic color.*

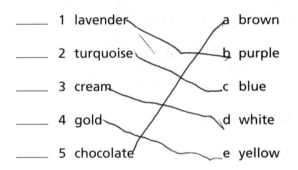

_____ 1 lavender   a brown

_____ 2 turquoise   b purple

_____ 3 cream   c blue

_____ 4 gold   d white

_____ 5 chocolate   e yellow

WARM-UP				
Number of correct answers	0–4	5–6	7–8	9–10
Neuro-points earned	0	1	2	3

To continue your WARM-UP, turn to page 132.

SOLUTIONS B 1b 2c 3d 4e 5a
             A 1d 2b 3e 4a 5c

Match the terms in the first column with those in the second.

A Match each dish with its country or area of origin.

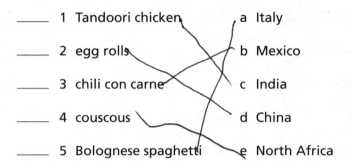

_____ 1 Tandoori chicken   a Italy

_____ 2 egg rolls   b Mexico

_____ 3 chili con carne   c India

_____ 4 couscous   d China

_____ 5 Bolognese spaghetti   e North Africa

B Match each physician with his or her specialty.

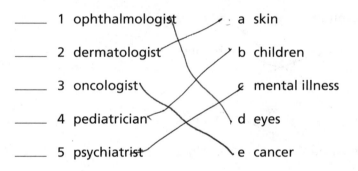

_____ 1 ophthalmologist   a skin

_____ 2 dermatologist   b children

_____ 3 oncologist   c mental illness

_____ 4 pediatrician   d eyes

_____ 5 psychiatrist   e cancer

CHALLENGE

Number of correct answers	0–4	5–6	7–8	9–10
Neuro-points earned	0	1	2	3

To continue your CHALLENGE, turn to page 135.

SOLUTIONS B 1d 2a 3e 4b 5c
A 1c 2d 3b 4e 5a

Match the terms in the first column with those in the second.

A *Match each bone with the part of the body in which it is located.*

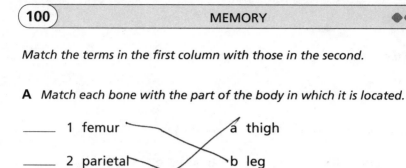

_____ 1 femur   a thigh

_____ 2 parietal   b leg

_____ 3 clavicle   c skull

_____ 4 tibia   d back

_____ 5 vertebra   e shoulder

B *Match each plant with the plant group to which it belongs.*

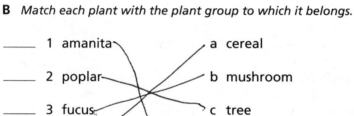

_____ 1 amanita   a cereal

_____ 2 poplar   b mushroom

_____ 3 fucus   c tree

_____ 4 corn   d herb

_____ 5 oregano   e alga

PRACTICE				
Number of correct answers	0–4	5–6	7–8	9–10
Neuro-points earned	0	1	2	3

To continue your PRACTICE, turn to page 131.

SOLUTIONS   B 1b 2c 3e 4a 5d
                     A 1a 2c 3e 4b 5d

Match the terms in the first column with those in the second.

A *Match each president with the year in which he was elected.*

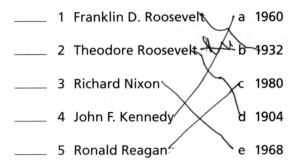

_____ 1 Franklin D. Roosevelt   a 1960

_____ 2 Theodore Roosevelt   b 1932

_____ 3 Richard Nixon   c 1980

_____ 4 John F. Kennedy   d 1904

_____ 5 Ronald Reagan   e 1968

B *Match each unit of measurement with what it measures.*

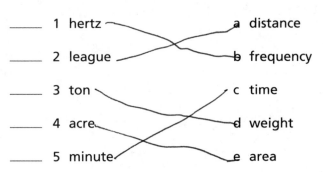

_____ 1 hertz   a distance

_____ 2 league   b frequency

_____ 3 ton   c time

_____ 4 acre   d weight

_____ 5 minute   e area

CHALLENGE				
Number of correct answers	0–4	5–6	7–8	9–10
Neuro-points earned	0	1	2	3

To continue your CHALLENGE, turn to page 133.

SOLUTIONS   A 1b 2d 3e 4a 5c
                  B 1b 2a 3d 4e 5c

LANGUAGE

Most people can read the following sentence and readily understand what it means: "And Little Red Riding Hood was eaten by the big, bad ... elephant!"

Our understanding of and ability to use language is a characteristic that differentiates us from other animals. However, reading is a complex mental task involving language comprehension and various types of analysis. For example, visual analysis enables you to determine that such and such a shape corresponds to a particular letter or word. Spelling analysis allows you to spot typographical errors. Syntactic analysis helps you to determine whether a sentence is grammatically correct. Phonologic analysis allows you to recognize the sound of a word, that is, how it is pronounced. You understand the meaning of words through semantic analysis.

Reading a word is made easier by several factors. The frequency rate of a certain word in a language plays a role in how it is read: the more frequently the word is used, the more easily it is identified. This may indicate that words are stored in our memory in an order that takes their frequency into account.

The meaning of a word in a sentence is also of great help while reading. When you read the beginning of a sentence and understand the words, you expect the following words to make sense in the context of the words already read. In the example above, after "big, bad," you probably expected "wolf," not "elephant."

The ease with which you read a word also depends on physical criteria. You're used to reading words with a specific physical shape; if this shape changes, you will read more slowly. For instance, if "elephant" is printed "eLePhAnT," your reading will slow down as your brain seeks to make sense of the different presentation.

Reading continuous text is a succession of steps, sentence after sentence, paragraph after paragraph. To understand such a text, you must keep in mind (temporarily) the information read in each sentence. This brings you to the next step: the next sentence or paragraph. Most people, however, cannot remember each sentence exactly as it appears in the text. Only the most relevant information is stored (and for a longer time). This enables you, for example, to write a summary. At the same time, irrelevant, redundant, and contradictory information is erased from your memory to avoid overload, since your ultimate goal is to determine the general meaning of the text.

In continuous text, words are organized in coherent structures. You extract a global meaning and link it to a central theme. Your general knowledge helps you to make sense of the text. For example, if you don't know the Little Red Riding Hood story, and if you don't know that elephants don't eat humans, the example above probably didn't seem strange to you.

If a particular text is not obviously coherent, you automatically make inferences based on your general knowledge of the world. For instance, if you read sentences that have no apparent link, such as "The car has been stolen. Paul has no money left," you may create an inference that gives coherence to the text: "All his money was in the car."

The four sets of exercises that follow deal with language.

- **Play with Haikus**, which trains your ability to analyze meaning and comprehend
- **Embroidery**, which trains you to carry out a lexical search in your vocabulary
- **Split Words**, which taps into your vocabulary, including words you hardly ever use and may forget
- **This Story Is Full of Blanks**, which sharpens your analysis of syntax and comprehension of text

Make your words count!

Play with Haikus

Text, even when presented as a poem, follows a logical succession. The exercises in this set will challenge your language abilities as you identify the purpose of a text, analyze its logic and grammar, and determine its poetic meaning.

You will be asked to identify which season of the year is implied in the haiku or to form a haiku from jumbled lines or words.

NOTE: These haikus don't follow the 5/7/5–syllable structure of traditional haikus, but they do use typical content and the customary three-line format.

Each of the five haikus below implies a particular season of the year.
Allow yourself 30 seconds to determine the implied seasons.

1 Constant wind
   The icicles more curved
   With each drip

   ☐ Spring
   ☐ Summer
   ☒ Fall
   ☐ Winter

2 Even if you are cold
   Do not go near the fire
   Little snowman

   ☒ Spring
   ☐ Summer
   ☐ Fall
   ☐ Winter

3 Quiet cove
   The sound of crow's feet
   Cracking thin ice

   ☒ Spring
   ☐ Summer
   ☐ Fall
   ☐ Winter

4 I swept the dead leaves
   The passersby
   Do not see it

   ☐ Spring
   ☐ Summer
   ☒ Fall
   ☐ Winter

5 Rain falls equally
   On plants, on stones, on soil
   Many flowers bloom

   ☐ Spring
   ☒ Summer
   ☐ Fall
   ☐ Winter

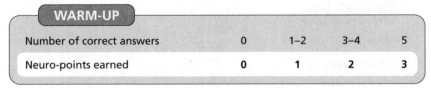

WARM-UP				
Number of correct answers	0	1–2	3–4	5
Neuro-points earned	0	1	2	3

To continue your WARM-UP, turn to page 141.

SOLUTIONS   1 winter 2 winter 3 winter 4 fall 5 spring

Each of the five haikus below implies a particular season of the year.
Allow yourself 30 seconds to determine the implied seasons.

1 Bushes by the roadway
   When you look closer
   Blossoming flowers

   ☐ Spring
   ☐ Summer
   ☐ Fall
   ☐ Winter

2 From which blooming tree
   I do not know
   What a perfume!

   ☐ Spring
   ☐ Summer
   ☐ Fall
   ☐ Winter

3 Snow-capped mountains
   My knucklebones as white
   As the surf

   ☐ Spring
   ☐ Summer
   ☐ Fall
   ☐ Winter

4 Hot days
   A dried earthworm
   On the road

   ☐ Spring
   ☐ Summer
   ☐ Fall
   ☐ Winter

5 The leaves fall
   The snail moves
   So slowly

   ☐ Spring
   ☐ Summer
   ☐ Fall
   ☐ Winter

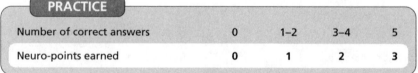

PRACTICE

Number of correct answers	0	1–2	3–4	5
Neuro-points earned	0	1	2	3

To continue your PRACTICE, turn to page 145.

SOLUTIONS 1 spring 2 spring 3 winter 4 summer 5 fall

In the five haikus below, the lines have been jumbled. Allow yourself 30 seconds to correctly order the lines. Using the line letters, write the correct sequence on the lines at the right.

1 a The snowball
   b At the end became
   c Round and huge

                 1
                 2
                 3

2 a A spring wind
   b Fly in a field like
   c Little birds sing and

                 3
                 2
                 1

3 a My feelings of tender love
   b Petals and
   c Have fallen

                 2
                 1
                 3

4 a When did you get here
   b Right at my feet
   c Snail?

             3   A
             1   B
             2   C

5 a A naked horse
   b Naked, I am riding under
   c A sudden shower, on

             3   C
             1   B
             2   A

WARM-UP

Number of haikus correctly ordered	0	1–2	3–4	5
Neuro-points earned	0	1	2	3

To continue your WARM-UP, turn to page 143.

SOLUTIONS 1 a-b-c 2 c-b-a 3 b-a-c 4 a-b-c 5 b-c-a

In the five haikus below, the lines have been jumbled. Allow yourself 30 seconds to correctly order the lines. Using the line letters, write the correct sequence on the lines at the right.

1 a Huge
   b The small fish
   c Eventually became

2 a Flutter their wings and
   b I watch two butterflies
   c Spread colors into the air

3 a I am writing in search
   b Divine grace
   c Of beauty and

4 a Is your body also
   b Green frog,
   c Freshly painted?

5 a In my old home
   b Are in bloom
   c Which I forsook, the cherries

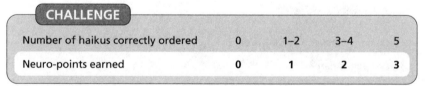

CHALLENGE

Number of haikus correctly ordered	0	1–2	3–4	5
Neuro-points earned	0	1	2	3

To continue your CHALLENGE, turn to page 147.

SOLUTIONS 1 b-c-a 2 b-a-c 3 a-c-b 4 b-a-c 5 a-c-b

*In the four haikus below, the words in each line have been jumbled.
Allow yourself 60 seconds to write the words in the correct order
on the blank lines below each haiku.*

1 palm I my opened and
lines its Traced
To life your where mine crosses

_____ _____ _____ _____ _____

_____ _____ _____

_____ _____ _____ _____ _____

2 Buddha in the A moor
nose of his end At the hangs
icicle An

_____ _____ _____ _____ _____

_____ _____ _____ _____ _____ _____ _____

_____ _____

3 mist In the
pine pretends tree A
To ghost be a

_____ _____ _____

_____ _____ _____ _____

_____ _____ _____ _____

4 A and drinks bear sees
reflection His in
lake The silent

_____ _____ _____ _____ _____

_____ _____ _____

_____ _____ _____

Turn the page for the solutions.

SOLUTIONS

1 I opened my palm and
   Traced its lines
   To where your life crosses mine

2 A Buddha in the moor
   At the end of his nose hangs
   An icicle

3 In the mist
   A pine tree pretends
   To be a ghost

4 A bear drinks and sees
   His reflection in
   The silent lake

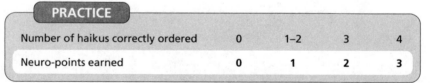

PRACTICE

Number of haikus correctly ordered	0	1–2	3	4
Neuro-points earned	0	1	2	3

To continue your PRACTICE, turn to page 142.

In the four haikus below, the words in each line have been jumbled.
Allow yourself 60 seconds to write the words in the correct order
on the blank lines below each haiku.

1 face I remember his and
   inclines The he head way his
   pass As I by

   _____ _____ _____ _____ _____

   _____ _____ _____ _____ _____

   _____ _____ _____ _____

2 the path Sensing
   to Leads the ant nowhere,
   lanes changes Quickly

   _____ _____ _____

   _____ _____ _____ _____ _____

   _____ _____ _____

3 what Poet, craziness
   you to Drove believe
   could stars? You the hold

   _____ _____ _____

   _____ _____ _____ _____

   _____ _____ _____ _____ _____

4 want I close to be
   Can I you To. tuck head my
   neck? Into your

   _____ _____ _____ _____ _____

   _____ _____ _____ _____ _____ _____ _____

   _____ _____ _____

Turn the page for the solutions.

SOLUTIONS

1　I remember his face and
　The way he inclines his head
　As I pass by

2　Sensing the path
　Leads to nowhere, the ant
　Quickly changes lanes

3　Poet, what craziness
　Drove you to believe
　You could hold the stars?

4　I want to be close
　To you. Can I tuck my head
　Into your neck?

CHALLENGE

Number of haikus correctly ordered	0	1–2	3	4
Neuro-points earned	0	1	2	3

To continue your CHALLENGE, turn to page 144.

Embroidery

Finding a word in a grid is relatively easy when you know what the word is. It is much more difficult when you don't know what the word is, and its seven, eight, or nine letters are hidden among other letters.

In this set of exercises, you will find words between seven and nine letters long in a letter grid. Letters of the word are sequentially arranged in horizontally or vertically, but not diagonally, contiguous squares. Each letter may be used only once. An example (for the word *assistant*) follows.

D	A	G	R
P	S	S	I
U	B	T	S
T	N	A	C

To earn the maximum number of neuro-points, complete the two exercises below in ten minutes or less.

A *Find a seven-letter word in the grid below. The first two letters of the word are in shaded squares.*

E	U	Q	T
I	L	X	T
B	R	E	R
L	T	C	A

B *Find a nine-letter word in the grid below. The first two letters of the word are in shaded squares.*

U	T	R	Y
O	S	I	T
H	Y	M	A
P	N	O	N

WARM-UP

If you answered in this amount of time ...	—	—	more than 10 minutes	less than 10 minutes
And you correctly identified this number of words ...	0	1	2	2
Neuro-points earned	0	1	2	3

To continue your WARM-UP, turn to page 150.

SOLUTIONS A extract B anonymity

*To earn the maximum number of neuro-points, complete the two
exercises below in ten minutes or less.*

A *Find a seven-letter word in the grid below. The first two letters
of the word are in shaded squares.*

B	O	M	C
A	N	T	Y
S	I	T	O
U	V	I	R

B *Find a nine-letter word in the grid below. The first two letters
of the word are in shaded squares.*

U	D	G	S
D	H	O	A
N	X	G	T
U	O	R	R

PRACTICE

If you answered in this amount of time ...	—	—	more than 10 minutes	less than 10 minutes
And you correctly identified this number of words ...	0	1	2	2
Neuro-points earned	0	1	2	3

To continue your PRACTICE, turn to page 154.

SOLUTIONS A *monitor* B *groundhog*

To earn the maximum number of neuro-points, complete the two exercises below in ten minutes or less.

A *Find an eight-letter word in the grid below. The word relates to* **family.**

T	E	S	T
N	C	H	O
A	C	T	R
J	I	N	A

B *Find a nine-letter word in the grid below. The word relates to* **occupation.**

C	A	R	R
O	E	P	F
T	N	T	E
P	A	R	R

WARM-UP

If you answered in this amount of time ...	—	—	more than 10 minutes	less than 10 minutes
And you correctly identified this number of words ...	0	1	2	2
Neuro-points earned	0	1	2	3

To continue your WARM-UP, turn to page 152.

SOLUTIONS A ancestor B carpenter

To earn the maximum number of neuro-points, complete the two exercises below in ten minutes or less.

A Find a seven-letter word in the grid below. The word relates to **astronomy.**

E	J	E	S
S	O	I	P
H	T	L	X
C	E	C	U

B Find a nine-letter word in the grid below. The word relates to **the night sky.**

M	O	E	Y
A	O	N	L
R	H	G	I
G	T	S	T

CHALLENGE

If you answered in this amount of time …	—	—	more than 10 minutes	less than 10 minutes
And you correctly identified this number of words …	0	1	2	2
Neuro-points earned	0	1	2	3

To continue your CHALLENGE, turn to page 155.

SOLUTIONS   A eclipse B moonlight

To earn the maximum number of neuro-points, complete the two exercises below in ten minutes or less.

A *Find a nine-letter word in the grid below.*

F	M	L	U
F	A	C	H
I	Y	R	I
R	N	E	N

B *Find a seven-letter word in the grid below.*

O	U	M	E
C	A	L	L
P	U	N	Y
H	E	D	R

PRACTICE

If you answered in this amount of time ...	—	—	more than 10 minutes	less than 10 minutes
And you correctly identified this number of words ...	0	1	2	2
Neuro-points earned	0	1	2	3

To continue your PRACTICE, turn to page 151.

SOLUTIONS   *A machinery B laundry*

To earn the maximum number of neuro-points, complete the two exercises below in ten minutes or less.

A *Find an eight-letter word in the grid below.*

K	L	A	W
P	R	S	E
P	A	I	D
A	S	H	E

B *Find a nine-letter word in the grid below.*

A	I	R	B
F	L	D	A
G	I	M	N
N	N	T	O

CHALLENGE

If you answered in this amount of time …	—	—	more than 10 minutes	less than 10 minutes
And you correctly identified this number of words …	0	1	2	2
Neuro-points earned	0	1	2	3

To continue your CHALLENGE, turn to page 153.

SOLUTIONS A sidewalk B badminton

Split Words

Every day you store words in your mind that you use later when you speak. In this set of exercises, you will jog your memory by playing with split words, combining them into whole words again as quickly as possible. You will be given a theme, as well as a syllable count, to guide you.

Allow yourself three minutes to combine the split words in the grid below into 20 whole words of one or two syllables. The theme is **clothes**.

Each grid item may be used only once.

tu	T-	cking	ment	sweat
ter	pon	bow	sers	swea
swim	se	coat	tie	ja
llar	be	jum	nim	dal
ro	de	glo	cket	sto
blou	tten	nic	trou	per
shirt	gar	san	mi	ve
suit	rain	co	cho	pants

Write the words you find below.

_____ _____ _____ _____

_____ _____ _____ _____

_____ _____ _____ _____

_____ _____ _____ _____

_____ _____ _____ _____

WARM-UP

Number of words found	0–5	6–11	12–16	17–20
Neuro-points earned	0	1	2	3

To continue your WARM-UP, turn to page 157.

SOLUTION blouse, bowtie, collar, denim, garment, glove, jacket, jumper, mitten, poncho, raincoat, robe, sandal, stocking, sweater, sweatpants, swimsuit, trousers, T-shirt, tunic

Allow yourself three minutes to combine the split words in the grid below into 20 whole words of one or two syllables. The theme is **dance**.

Each grid item may be used only once.

tan	tu	po	lo	thm
sce	mam	go	trot	tem
llet	go	rum	go-	ge
room	ba	foot	hop	pol
sal	pper	rhy	so	cha
work	tu	fox-	sa	ba
ball	sta	cha	hip-	ne
te	ka	poin	bo	sli

Write the words you find below.

_____ _____ _____ _____

_____ _____ _____ _____

_____ _____ _____ _____

_____ _____ _____ _____

_____ _____ _____ _____

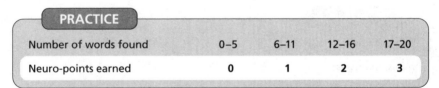

PRACTICE

Number of words found	0–5	6–11	12–16	17–20
Neuro-points earned	0	1	2	3

To continue your PRACTICE, turn to page 161.

SOLUTION   ballet, ballroom, chacha, footwork, fox-trot, go-go,
hip-hop, mambo, pointe, polka, rhythm, rumba, salsa,
scene, slipper, solo, stage, tango, tempo, tutu

Allow yourself five minutes to combine the split words in the grid below into 20 whole words of two, three, or four syllables. The theme is **emotions and feelings**.

Each grid item may be used only once.

des	sen	dread	ment	tion	ness
fflic	sur	ffec	ce	ge	sy
pa	der	out	tas	ness	ti
cou	eu	ha	mo	su	te
a	plea	jea	mi	ry	a
se	ge	lou	ve	se	ful
de	ra	duc	re	tion	si
ry	bra	sen	pri	tien	tion
ria	sa	se	ness	ty	ppi
ten	dis	tion	ra	re	pho

Write the words you find below.

_____ _____ _____

_____ _____ _____

_____ _____ _____

_____ _____ _____

_____ _____ _____

WARM-UP

Number of words found	0–5	6–11	12–16	17–20
Neuro-points earned	0	1	2	3

To continue your WARM-UP, turn to page 159.

SOLUTION

affection, affliction, bravery, courage, desire, distaste, dreadfulness, euphoria, happiness, jealousy, misery, modesty, outrage, patience, pleasure, seduction, sensation, sentiment, surprise, tenderness

Allow yourself five minutes to combine the split words in the grid below into 20 whole words of two or three syllables. The theme is **animals**.

Each grid item may be used only once.

kan	bird	ter	qui	na	re
a	ffe	tu	ga	vy	ve
ea	zee	goo	o	le	pe
phant	to	le	lo	e	la
an	ri	li	to	ca	too
e	ko	ri	ry	gi	mon
lla	can	hy	bou	bu	pus
ant	cka	vul	cho	go	lo
ca	se	chim	pard	ra	ffa
oc	co	na	mos	pan	roo

Write the words you find below.

_____ _____ _____ _____

_____ _____ _____ _____

_____ _____ _____ _____

_____ _____ _____ _____

_____ _____ _____

To continue your CHALLENGE, turn to page 162.

CHALLENGE

Number of words found	0–5	6–11	12–16	17–20
Neuro-points earned	0	1	2	3

SOLUTION anchovy, anteater, buffalo, canary, caribou, chimpanzee, cockatoo, elephant, giraffe, gorilla, hyena, kangaroo, koala, leopard, lovebird, mongoose, mosquito, octopus, pelican, vulture

Allow yourself five minutes to combine the split words in the grid below into 20 whole words of three or four syllables. The theme is **trades and occupations**.

Each grid item may be used only once.

en	cist	neer	si	list	son
cian	sult	ant	ccount	ssor	gner
na	o	ant	jour	li	ter
ger	lyst	pro	re	na	rian
the	ins	ra	pec	pist	na
a	con	ar	di	ant	gi
pen	a	ssist	car	ffi	ma
ma	sear	tech	de	ni	bra
a	phar	bell	chi	cher	per
tor	cer	rec	fe	tect	tor

Write the words you find below.

_____ _____ _____ _____

_____ _____ _____ _____

_____ _____ _____ _____

_____ _____ _____ _____

_____ _____ _____ _____

To continue your PRACTICE, turn to page 158.

SOLUTION   accountant, analyst, architect, assistant, bellperson, carpenter, consultant, designer, director, engineer, inspector, journalist, librarian, manager, officer, pharmacist, professor, researcher, technician, therapist

Allow yourself five minutes to combine the split words in the grid below into 20 whole words of two or three syllables. The theme is **war materiel and weapons**.

Each grid item may be used only once.

ka	arm	net	de	rine	bi
ba	jec	zoo	car	ver	nis
sub	tur	ca	gun	ssi	ter
smooth	gun	re	ma	bo	lin
pult	yo	trid	llant	ne	fi
der	pro	ta	re	le	ba
pe	try	car	tor	fan	pro
ve	gre	re	mi	ge	in
bo	do	ca	vol	re	pow
tile	fi	na	ja	pe	jet

Write the words you find below.

_____   _____   _____   _____

_____   _____   _____   _____

_____   _____   _____   _____

_____   _____   _____   _____

_____   _____   _____   _____

CHALLENGE

Number of words found	0–5	6–11	12–16	17–20
Neuro-points earned	0	1	2	3

To continue your CHALLENGE, turn to page 160.

SOLUTION bayonet, bazooka, canister, carbine, cartridge, catapult, firearm, grenade, gunfire, gunpowder, infantry, javelin, missile, projectile, propellant, revolver, smoothbore, submarine, torpedo, turbojet

This Story Is Full of Blanks

In a noisy room, you can often determine the basic meaning of a conversation by putting together the bits and pieces you hear. Similarly, when you read a passage in a foreign language, translating key words is often enough to discern the general meaning.

In this set of exercises, you will analyze text and supply missing words by deduction and by drawing on your knowledge of grammar.

Read the following selection from F. Scott Fitzgerald's The Great Gatsby. *Allow yourself three minutes to supply the missing words from the list below.*

I _____ from the station directly to Gatsby's

_____ and my rushing _____ up the front

steps was the first _____ that _____ anyone.

But they knew then, I firmly _____. With scarcely a

_____ said, four of us, the chauffeur, _____,

gardener and I, _____ down to the pool. There was

a _____, barely perceptible movement of the

_____ as the fresh _____ from one end

urged its way _____ the drain at the other. With little

_____ that were hardly the shadows of waves, the

_____ mattress moved irregularly down the pool.

faint	alarmed	believe	water	flow
butler	hurried	drove	thing	house
toward	ripples	word	laden	anxiously

WARM-UP

Number of correct words	0–5	6–9	10–14	15
Neuro-points earned	0	1	2	3

To continue your WARM-UP, turn to page 164.

SOLUTION   drove, house, anxiously, thing, alarmed, believe, word, butler, hurried, faint, water, flow, toward, ripples, laden

Read the following selection. Allow yourself three minutes to supply the missing words from the list below.

Once upon a _____ there was a king who had a

_____ who was very fond of hunting. The king often

_____ him to indulge in this pastime, but he had

_____ his minister always to go with _____

and never to lose _____ of him. One _____

the huntsman roused a _____, and the prince,

_____ that the minister was _____ him,

gave chase, and rode so _____ that he found himself

alone. He _____, and having lost sight of the stag,

turned to _____ the minister, who had not been

_____ enough to follow him. But the minister had

lost his _____.

day	rejoin	ordered	sight	careful
son	stag	hard	time	thinking
way	behind	him	stopped	allowed

To continue your PRACTICE, turn to page 168.

SOLUTION time, son, allowed, ordered, him, sight, day, stag, thinking, behind, hard, stopped, rejoin, careful, way

Read the following selection. Allow yourself three minutes to supply the missing words from the list below.

His _____ over, Professor Ainslie Grey paid a

_____ to his laboratory, where he adjusted several

_____ instruments, made a note as to the

_____ of three separate infusions of _____,

and resolved the questions of seven different _____,

who were pursuing research in as many _____ lines

of inquiry. _____ thus conscientiously and

_____ completed his _____, he returned

to his carriage and ordered the _____ to drive him to

The Lindens. His _____ was cold and impassive, but he

_____ his fingers from time to _____ down

his prominent _____ with a jerky, twitchy movement.

face	visit	bacteria	time	duties
separate	coachman	Having	lecture	methodically
drew	scientific	students	chin	progress

WARM-UP

Number of correct words	0–5	6–9	10–14	15
Neuro-points earned	0	1	2	3

To continue your WARM-UP, turn to page 166.

SOLUTION   lecture, visit, scientific, progress, bacteria, students, separate, Having, methodically, duties, coachman, face, drew, time, chin

Read the following selection. Allow yourself three minutes to supply the missing words from the list below.

More than an _____ after this, he stood in

the _____ of Doctor Jeltry's suburban residence.

He _____ induced a juvenile maidservant to let

the _____ know that he was there. She had

_____, after a long absence, to say that

_____ Jeltry would come down to him in a

little _____. He took a nearby book and spent ten

_____ flipping through it. Then he threw it down.

There was no _____ book to be seen,

and he had _____ read the magazines; so there was

_____ for him to do. The occupants of the house

still _____ to appear. He could only stare

_____ him, into the bright, bare _____

room, which was so hot that he wished to _____

a window.

had	nothing	other	minutes	Miss
failed	returned	before	hour	common
ladies	already	parlor	open	while

CHALLENGE

Number of correct words	0–5	6–9	10–14	15
Neuro-points earned	0	1	2	3

To continue your CHALLENGE, turn to page 169.

SOLUTION hour, parlor, had, ladies, returned, Miss, while, minutes, other, already, nothing, failed, before, common, open

Read the following selection from Alfred, Lord Tennyson's poem "Break, Break, Break." Allow yourself three minutes to supply the missing words from the list below.

Break, _____, break

On _____ cold grey stones, O _____!

_____ I would that my _____ could utter

The _____ that arise in me.

O _____ for the fisherman's _____,

That he _____ with _____ sister at play!

O well _____ the sailor lad,

That he sings in his _____ on the _____!

And the stately ships _____ on

To their haven _____ the hill …

go	his	break	boy	And
tongue	shouts	well	boat	under
thoughts	bay	thy	for	Sea

PRACTICE

Number of correct words	0–5	6–9	10–14	15
Neuro-points earned	0	1	2	3

To continue your PRACTICE, turn to page 165.

SOLUTION break, thy, Sea, And, tongue, thoughts, well, boy, shouts, his, for, boat, bay, go, under.

*Read the following selection from Henry Wadsworth Longfellow's poem
"A Psalm of Life." Allow yourself three minutes to supply the missing
words from the list below.*

Tell _____ not, in mournful numbers,

_____ is but an _____ dream!

For the _____ is dead that _____,

And _____ are not what they _____.

Life is _____! Life _____ earnest!

And the grave is not its _____;

_____ thou art, to dust _____,

_____ not spoken of the soul.

Not enjoyment, and not _____,

Is our _____ end or way …

me	Dust	slumbers	destined	empty
sorrow	seem	Life	is	goal
returnest	Was	real	soul	things

CHALLENGE

Number of correct words	0–5	6–9	10–14	15
Neuro-points earned	0	1	2	3

To continue your CHALLENGE, turn to page 167.

SOLUTION   me, Life, empty, soul, slumbers, things, seem, real,
is, goal, Dust, returnest, Was, sorrow, destined

VISUAL AND SPATIAL ACUITY

Imagine four objects of various shapes: a pyramid, two cubes, and a sphere. If you are asked to grasp the cube nearest the pyramid, you'll have no difficulty in carrying out the task. This apparently simple task, however, uses complex cognitive processes. For example, successful completion of this task requires recognition of the four objects in order to differentiate the cubes from the other objects. After determining that there are only two cubes, you decide which one is closest to the pyramid by mentally evaluating the distance between each cube and the pyramid.

Every day you are faced with similar situations that require recognition of visual shapes, analysis of one object's position in relation to another object (on its left or its right, above or below, in front of or behind), and/or evaluation of the distance between two objects (in inches, feet, or meters).

Our visual system is responsible for these spontaneous analyses. More precisely, two areas of the brain process such information: one area determines the shape of objects, and the other determines their spatial properties (such as size, location, and orientation).

Vision is a complex cognitive function—and a useful one too! It enables you to organize the huge amount of visual information that reaches your eyes into a coherent visual scene. It also enables you to identify the various objects that constitute your environment and their position in relation to other objects, yourself, and other people. Only then does interaction with your environment become possible: you can grasp objects, orient yourself, and so on.

Objects in your environment, therefore, are landmarks that enable you to orient yourself in space. To do so correctly, however, you also need information about your body, such as the current position of your arm or hand, and about the interaction of your body with the environment, so that you know what gesture or motion you can make to grasp an object. In the same way, when you drive somewhere, you view elements in the scenery and your brain creates mental maps that will (hopefully) enable you to effortlessly drive there again.

Back to our earlier example: Now imagine that someone asks you which cube would be closest to the pyramid if one cube was drawn three inches toward it. This requires that you mentally move the cube a distance you think is three inches, and then make a decision about the closest cube.

This process calls upon your capacity for mental imagery, a cognitive activity that enables you to perceive something when this something is not present or not happening. You "see" something in your mind. Visual analysis and mental imagery have numerous similarities, but only mental imagery allows you to transform an object—for instance, to rotate it—in your imagination.

Chess players frequently use mental imagery to evaluate the consequences of possible moves as they mentally simulate moving a piece without actually touching it. Mental imagery goes by other names, such as dreaming, reasoning, and mental calculation.

The exercises in this section help to train your perception of space and stimulate your capacity for mental imagery.

- **Entangled Figures**, which teaches you to recognize shapes and extract the shape of individual figures among other figures
- **Sleight of Hands**, which enhances your skills in visual rotation and mental imagery
- **Points of View**, which trains your mind to orient yourself in a given space
- **Mosaics**, which uses your visual analysis to engage in mental rotation, one of the most sophisticated mental operations

Open your eyes and get started!

Entangled Figures

When you see a familiar object, your mind subconsciously uses highly sophisticated intellectual mechanisms. You compare its shape with similar shapes in your memory, as well as numerous combinations of size, orientation, position, and color. Recognition becomes more complicated when you see an object out of context or when several shapes are superimposed on each other. The exercises in this section will develop your ability to distinguish shapes when they are superimposed on each other.

In 20 seconds or less, examine the figure below, then determine which three of the nine figures below it are combined to form the figure.

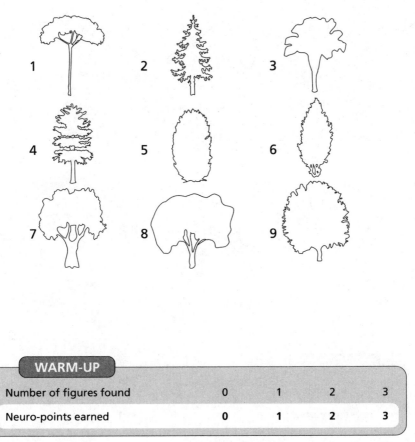

To continue your WARM-UP, turn to page 175.

WARM-UP				
Number of figures found	0	1	2	3
Neuro-points earned	0	1	2	3

SOLUTION   3, 5, and 8

In 20 seconds or less, examine the figure below, then determine which three of the nine figures below it are combined to form the figure.

1   2   3

4   5   6

  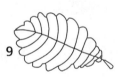

7   8   9

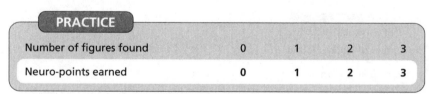

PRACTICE

Number of figures found	0	1	2	3
Neuro-points earned	0	1	2	3

To continue your PRACTICE, turn to page 179.

SOLUTION   2, 7, and 8

In 20 seconds or less, examine the figure below, then determine which three of the nine figures below it are combined to form the figure.

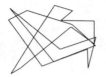

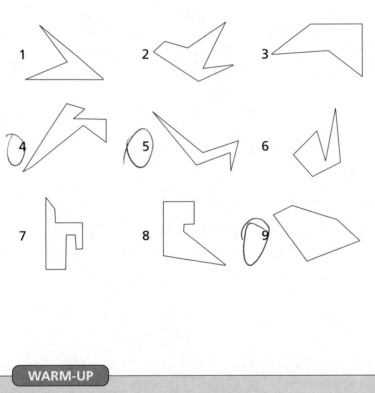

To continue your WARM-UP, turn to page 177.

WARM-UP				
Number of figures found	0	1	2	3
Neuro-points earned	0	1	2	3

SOLUTION　　*4, 5, and 9*

In 20 seconds or less, examine the figure below, then determine which three of the nine figures below it are combined to form the figure.

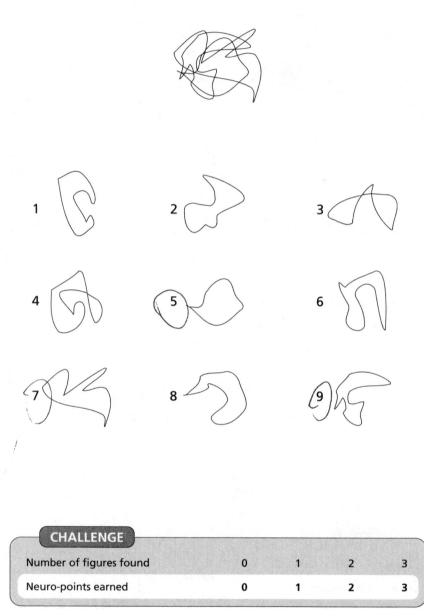

To continue your CHALLENGE, turn to page 180.

CHALLENGE

Number of figures found	0	1	2	3
Neuro-points earned	0	1	2	3

SOLUTION *5, 7, and 9*

Examine the figure below, then turn the page.

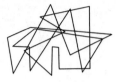

In 20 seconds or less, determine which three of the nine figures below are combined to form the figure on the preceding page.

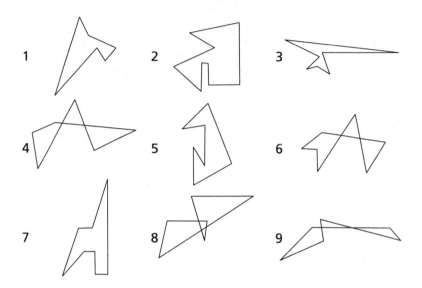

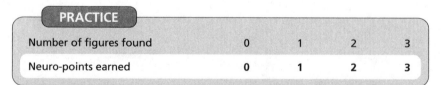

To continue your PRACTICE, turn to page 176.

SOLUTION   2, 4, and 6

Examine the figure below, then turn the page.

In 20 seconds or less, determine which three of the nine figures below are combined to form the figure on the preceding page.

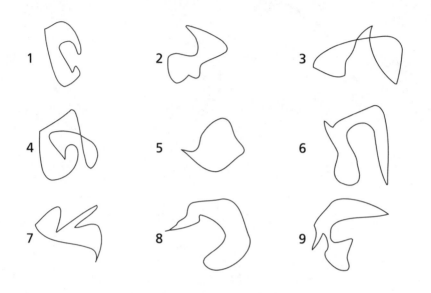

1

2

3

4

5

6

7

8

9

CHALLENGE

Number of figures found	0	1	2	3
Neuro-points earned	0	1	2	3

To continue your CHALLENGE, turn to page 178.

SOLUTION 2, 5, and 8

Sleight of Hands

Many of our daily mental tasks call upon our capacity for mental imagery. We're able to visualize a move before making it, mentally rotate an object to identify it, compare the shapes of objects, and so on.

In this set of exercises, you will use these abilities to determine whether the hand pictured is a right or left hand. Some of the pictures show hands viewed in a mirror; these pictures have scalloped corners and a reflective background.

A *Here are pictures of six hands. In one minute or less, determine whether each picture shows a right or left hand.*

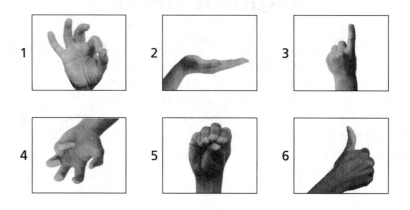

B *Here are pictures of hands holding objects. In one minute or less, determine whether each picture shows a right or left hand.*

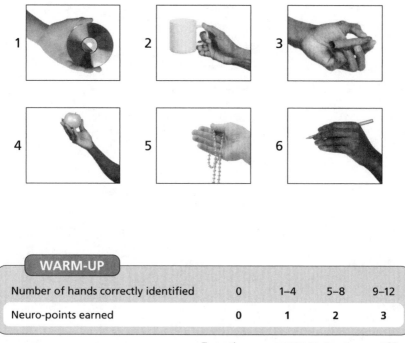

To continue your WARM-UP, turn to page 182.

WARM-UP

Number of hands correctly identified	0	1–4	5–8	9–12
Neuro-points earned	0	1	2	3

SOLUTIONS
A 1 right 2 right 3 left 4 left 5 right 6 right
B 1 left 2 right 3 left 4 right 5 right 6 left

A *Here are pictures of six hands. In one minute or less, determine whether each picture shows a right or left hand.*

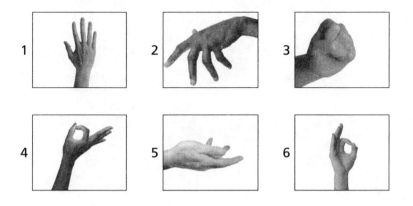

B *Here are pictures of hands holding objects. In one minute or less, determine whether each picture shows a right or left hand.*

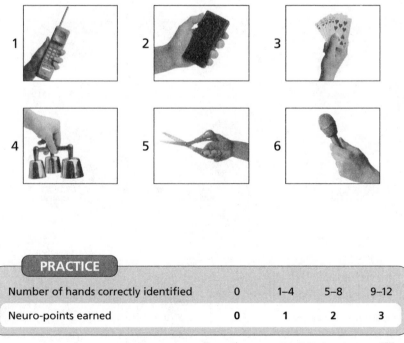

PRACTICE				
Number of hands correctly identified	0	1–4	5–8	9–12
Neuro-points earned	0	1	2	3

To continue your PRACTICE, turn to page 186.

SOLUTIONS   A 1 right 2 left 3 left 4 right 5 right 6 right
B 1 left 2 left 3 right 4 left 5 right 6 left

A *Here are pictures of six hands **viewed in a mirror**. In one minute or less, determine whether each picture shows a right or left hand.*

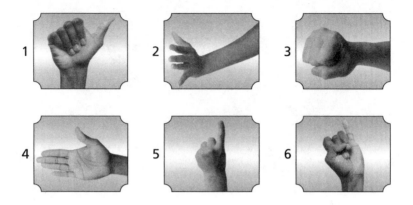

B *Here are pictures of six hands **viewed in a mirror** while holding objects. In one minute or less, determine whether each picture shows a right or left hand.*

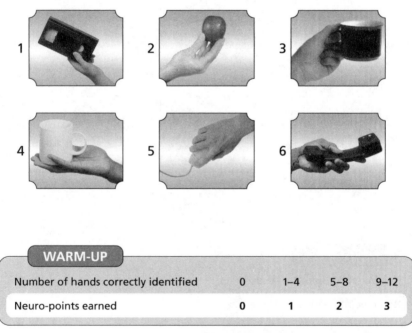

<table>
<thead>
<tr><th colspan="2">WARM-UP</th><th></th><th></th><th></th><th></th></tr>
</thead>
<tbody>
<tr><td>Number of hands correctly identified</td><td></td><td>0</td><td>1–4</td><td>5–8</td><td>9–12</td></tr>
<tr><td>Neuro-points earned</td><td></td><td>0</td><td>1</td><td>2</td><td>3</td></tr>
</tbody>
</table>

To continue your WARM-UP, turn to page 184.

SOLUTIONS **A** 1 left 2 right 3 left 4 left 5 right 6 right
B 1 right 2 left 3 right 4 left 5 left 6 right

A *Here are pictures of six hands **viewed in a mirror**. In one minute or less, determine whether each picture shows a right or left hand.*

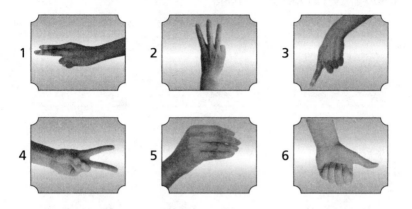

B *Here are pictures of six hands **viewed in a mirror** while holding objects. In one minute or less, determine whether each picture shows a right or left hand.*

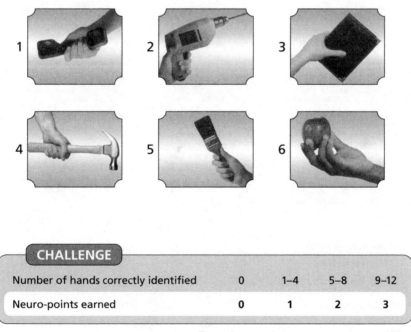

CHALLENGE

Number of hands correctly identified	0	1–4	5–8	9–12
Neuro-points earned	0	1	2	3

To continue your CHALLENGE, turn to page 187.

SOLUTIONS   **B** *1 left 2 right 3 right 4 right 5 left 6 left*
A *1 right 2 left 3 right 4 right 5 left 6 right*

A   *Here are pictures of six hands; some of the hands are **viewed in a mirror**, some are not. In one minute or less, determine whether each picture shows a right or left hand.*

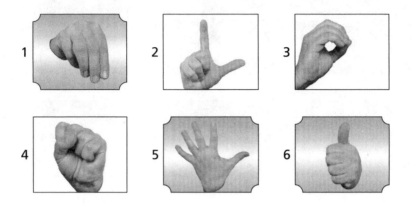

B   *Here are pictures of six hands holding objects; some of the hands are **viewed in a mirror**, some are not. In one minute or less, determine whether each picture shows a right or left hand.*

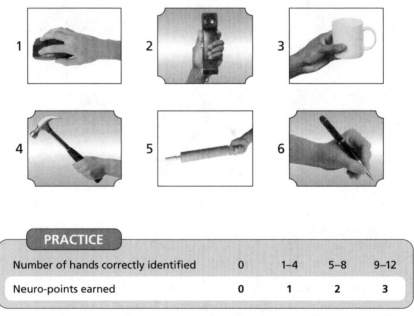

PRACTICE

Number of hands correctly identified	0	1–4	5–8	9–12
Neuro-points earned	0	1	2	3

To continue your PRACTICE, turn to page 183.

SOLUTIONS   A 1 left 2 right 3 right 4 left 5 right 6 right

B 1 right 2 right 3 left 4 right 5 right 6 right

A *Here are pictures of six hands; some of the hands are **viewed in a mirror**, some are not. In one minute or less, determine whether each picture shows a right or left hand.*

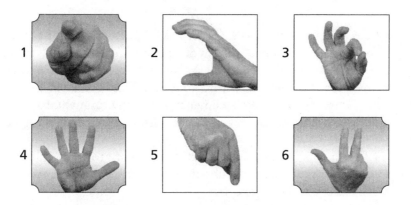

B *Here are pictures of six hands holding objects; some of the hands are **viewed in a mirror**, some are not. In one minute or less, determine whether each picture shows a right or left hand.*

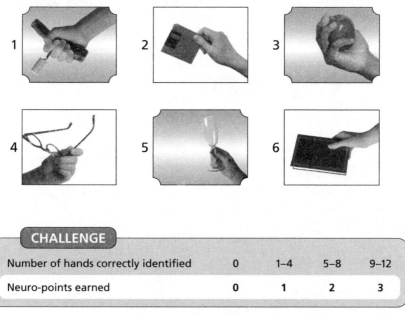

CHALLENGE

Number of hands correctly identified	0	1–4	5–8	9–12
Neuro-points earned	0	1	2	3

To continue your CHALLENGE, turn to page 185.

SOLUTIONS

B 1 left 2 right 3 left 4 left 5 left 6 right

A 1 right 2 left 3 left 4 left 5 right 6 left

Points of View

It is not easy to develop a three-dimensional representation of a landscape from a map, or to determine your position on a map based on the three-dimensional elements you see around you. To perform these operations effectively, you call upon your visual and spatial skills—to establish relationships between elements in the environment, to coordinate various points of view, to evaluate distances, and to focus on visual elements.

The following exercises will enhance your ability to position yourself in various locations; you will determine which position enables you to see the proposed perspective.

Examine this landscape.

The image below shows the landscape as seen from above. Determine where you would stand in the scenery to view the landscape as it appears in the top image. Try to do this in 45 seconds.

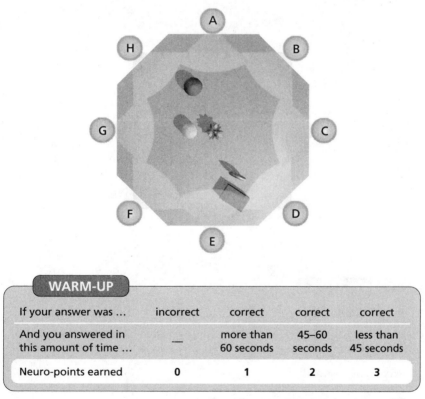

To continue your WARM-UP, turn to page 189.

WARM-UP			
If your answer was ...	incorrect	correct	correct	correct
And you answered in this amount of time ...	—	more than 60 seconds	45–60 seconds	less than 45 seconds
Neuro-points earned	0	1	2	3

SOLUTION *The scenery is viewed from point D.*

Examine this landscape.

The image below shows the landscape as seen from above. Determine where you would stand in the scenery to view the landscape as it appears in the top image. Try to do this in 45 seconds.

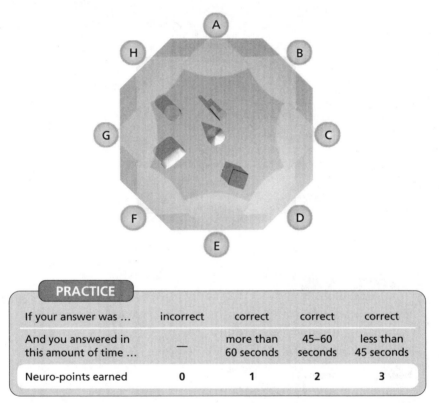

To continue your PRACTICE, turn to page 193.

PRACTICE				
If your answer was ...	incorrect	correct	correct	correct
And you answered in this amount of time ...	—	more than 60 seconds	45–60 seconds	less than 45 seconds
Neuro-points earned	0	1	2	3

SOLUTION *The scenery is viewed from point D.*

Examine this landscape.

The image below shows the landscape as seen from above. Determine where you would stand in the scenery to view the landscape as it appears in the top image. Try to do this in 45 seconds.

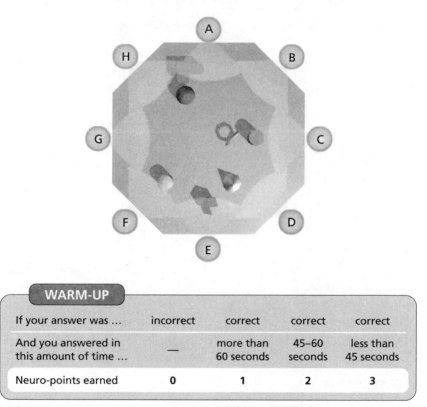

WARM-UP

If your answer was ...	incorrect	correct	correct	correct
And you answered in this amount of time ...	—	more than 60 seconds	45–60 seconds	less than 45 seconds
Neuro-points earned	0	1	2	3

To continue your WARM-UP, turn to page 191.

SOLUTION   *The scenery is viewed from point E.*

Examine this landscape.

The image below shows the landscape as seen from above. Determine where you would stand in the scenery to view the landscape as it appears in the top image. Try to do this in 45 seconds.

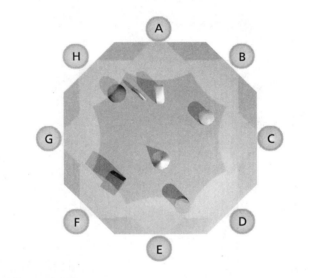

To continue your CHALLENGE, turn to page 194.

CHALLENGE

If your answer was ...	incorrect	correct	correct	correct
And you answered in this amount of time ...	—	more than 60 seconds	45–60 seconds	less than 45 seconds
Neuro-points earned	0	1	2	3

SOLUTION   *The scenery is viewed from point H.*

Examine this landscape.

The image below shows the landscape as seen from above. Determine where you would stand in the scenery to view the landscape as it appears in the top image. Try to do this in 45 seconds.

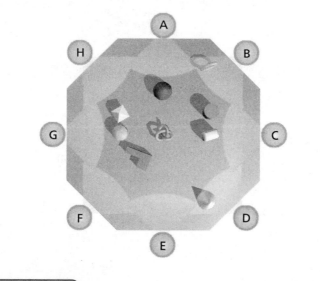

To continue your PRACTICE, turn to page 190.

PRACTICE				
If your answer was ...	incorrect	correct	correct	correct
And you answered in this amount of time ...	—	more than 60 seconds	45–60 seconds	less than 45 seconds
Neuro-points earned	0	1	2	3

SOLUTION   *The scenery is viewed from point G.*

Examine this landscape.

The image below shows the landscape as seen from above. Determine where you would stand in the scenery to view the landscape as it appears in the top image. Try to do this in 45 seconds.

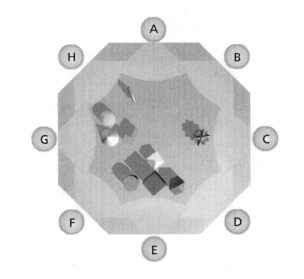

To continue your CHALLENGE, turn to page 192.

CHALLENGE

If your answer was ...	incorrect	correct	correct	correct
And you answered in this amount of time ...	—	more than 60 seconds	45–60 seconds	less than 45 seconds
Neuro-points earned	0	1	2	3

SOLUTION   *The scenery is viewed from point H.*

Mosaics

You may find it easy to put together a puzzle by physically manipulating the pieces. However, it is more difficult to determine if certain "pieces" belong in a picture just by moving them around in your mind.

In this set of exercises, you will determine if the figures in individual squares are the ones that make up a composite mosaic. A square may be rotated, as in a jigsaw puzzle, but it may not be flipped left to right or top to bottom.

In one minute or less, determine if the individual squares are found in the composite mosaic.

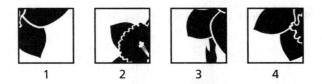

1 2 3 4

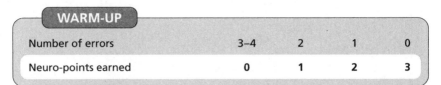

WARM-UP

Number of errors	3–4	2	1	0
Neuro-points earned	0	1	2	3

To continue your WARM-UP, turn to page 196.

SOLUTION *Square 3 is not used in the mosaic.*

In one minute or less, determine if the individual squares are found in the composite mosaic.

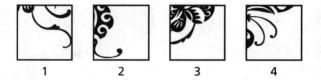

1	2	3	4

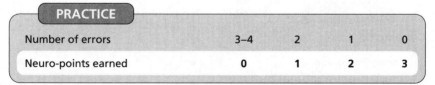

To continue your PRACTICE, turn to page 200.

SOLUTION   All squares are used in the mosaic.

In one minute or less, determine if the individual squares are found in the composite mosaic.

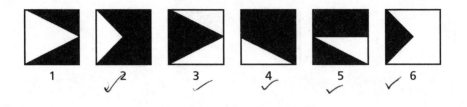

1   2   3   4   5   6

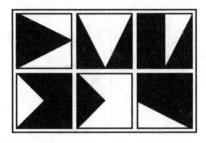

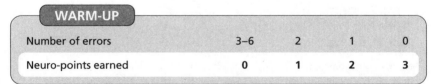

To continue your WARM-UP, turn to page 198.

SOLUTION *All squares are used in the mosaic.*

In one minute or less, determine if the individual squares are found in the composite mosaic.

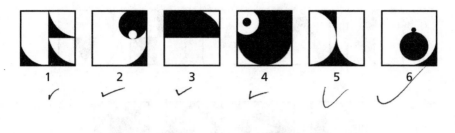

1   2   3   4   5   6

CHALLENGE

Number of errors	3–6	2	1	0
Neuro-points earned	0	1	2	3

To continue your CHALLENGE, turn to page 201.

SOLUTION   *Squares 1 and 2 are not used in the mosaic.*

In one minute or less, determine if the individual squares are found in the composite mosaic.

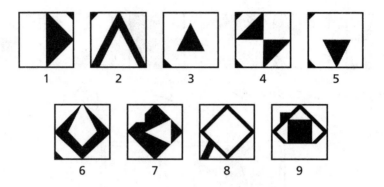

To continue your PRACTICE, turn to page 197.

PRACTICE

Number of errors	3–9	2	1	0
Neuro-points earned	0	1	2	3

SOLUTION　*Squares 4, 6, and 9 are not used in the mosaic.*

In one minute or less, determine if the individual squares are found in the composite mosaic.

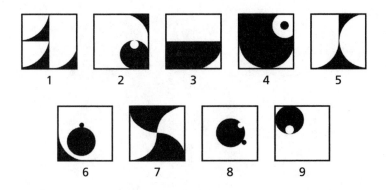

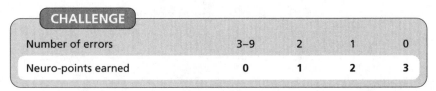

To continue your CHALLENGE, turn to page 199.

SOLUTION   Squares 3, 4, and 6 are not used in the mosaic.

REASONING

In daily life, you are often confronted with new and complex situations: planning the best itinerary for a trip, planning gardening chores according to the season, deciding the best strategy to get a promotion at work. To perform these tasks, you employ one or a combination of three different reasoning skills, depending on the situation.

Inferential reasoning comes into play when you're facing a problem that you've never encountered before and for which you have no immediate solution in memory. It is necessary to consider all the elements of the problem and to create hypotheses that may result, through deduction and inference, in a solution.

Analogical reasoning involves applying a solution that you have used before when faced with a similar problem.

Automatic reasoning is the spontaneous application of a known process. It occurs in familiar situations, such as when you are driving home. Automatic patterns are "stored" in procedural memory, from which you retrieve them when the same situation occurs again, such as riding a bicycle, driving a car, or playing the piano. Since the situation is not new, it does not require much attention, with the result that your mind may "wander."

Several steps are necessary for your brain to reason successfully. After analyzing a problem and defining your goal, you must determine a strategy and an action plan to solve the problem and reach your goal. If the goal is too difficult to reach in a single step, you must define intermediate objectives to make progress easier. At the same time, it is necessary to take into account the means available to you and to consider the constraints and processes that follow. Finally, it is crucial to select an appropriate solution when several solutions are available, and to make sure that your action plan will indeed achieve your goal.

Reasoning brings together the cognitive skills discussed in earlier sections of this book:

- *Attention.* To solve a problem, you need to focus on all the available information and determine which facts are most relevant. This determination enables you to clearly identify your goal and the strategy needed to reach it. Being focused also enables you to put aside obstacles that may disturb the problem-solving process. It may also help your brain block out unhelpful automatic responses.
- *Memory.* Long-term memory is often a critical part of reasoning. Indeed, you may rely on action plans already stored in memory to solve a new problem. Temporary memory, which stores a limited amount of information for a short period of time (on average, about seven items for 60 seconds), enables you to keep in mind the impor-

tant elements, such as the goal to achieve or a series of numbers, while you carry out a mental calculation.

- *Language.* When you formulate a hypothesis while reasoning, it is usually expressed through language (mental, written, or oral). Reasoning relies on language to give meaning to issues and then to analyze them.
- *Visual and spatial acuity.* Mental imagery is also a helpful tool in reasoning. It enables you to create, imagine, anticipate, compare, and mentally move ideas or objects around as you determine whether they can assist you in solving the problem at hand.

As you have worked on developing skills in these areas, you have been sharpening your reasoning skills. The exercises that follow will help you sharpen your reasoning skills even further.

- **Decipher**, in which you make hypotheses and deductions as a basis for reasoning
- **Writing in the Stars**, in which you analyze combinations of words that fit a given pattern
- **Towers of Hanoi**, which sharpens your ability to make mental calculations and plan strategies
- **Hurray for Change**, in which you move back and forth between two themes without becoming confused

Your turn to play!

Decipher

Deciphering ancient scripts and codes is a fascinating subject. In the following exercises, you will draw upon your concentration, language, and logic skills to decipher a quotation whose letters have been replaced by symbols.

The following hints may be helpful.

- A single-letter word is likely to be *a* or *I*.
- The most common letter at the end of a word is *e*.
- The most frequent letters in the English language are *e, t, a, i, o, n,* and *s*.
- The most frequent two-letter words are *of, to, in,* and *it*.
- The most common double-letter combinations are *ll, ee, ss, oo, tt, ff, rr, nn, pp,* and *cc*.

Decipher the two quotations below. The word given as the topic appears in the quotation. The quotations do not use the same code. Try to decipher both quotations in 10 minutes or less.

A *The following quotation about **life** is from Frank Lloyd Wright.*

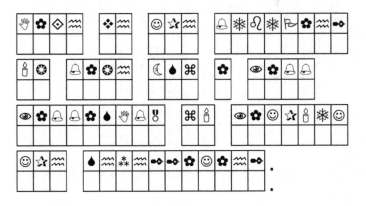

B *The following quotation about **love** is from D. H. Lawrence.*

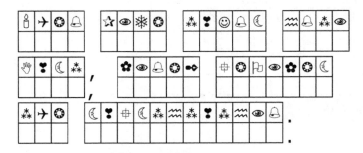

If you deciphered this number of quotations ...	0	1	2	2
And your time was ...	—	—	more than 10 minutes	less than 10 minutes
Neuro-points earned	0	1	2	3

WARM-UP

To continue your WARM-UP, turn to page 19.

SOLUTIONS

A *Give me the luxuries of life and I will willingly do without the necessities.*

B *When love turns into dust, money becomes the substitution.*

Decipher the two quotations below. The word given as the topic
appears in the quotation. The quotations do not use the same code.
Try to decipher both quotations in 10 minutes or less.

A The following quotation about **excess** is from Oscar Wilde.

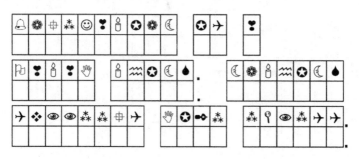

B The following quotation about being **rude** is from Rita May Brown.

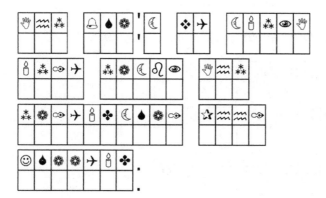

To continue your PRACTICE, turn to page 13.

SOLUTIONS B You can't be truly rude until you understand good manners.
A Moderation is a fatal thing. Nothing succeeds like excess.

Decipher the two quotations below. The white boxes signify vowels, and the shaded boxes signify consonants. The quotations do not use the same code. Try to decipher both quotations in 10 minutes or less.

A The following quotation is from Oscar Wilde.

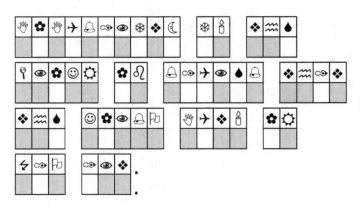

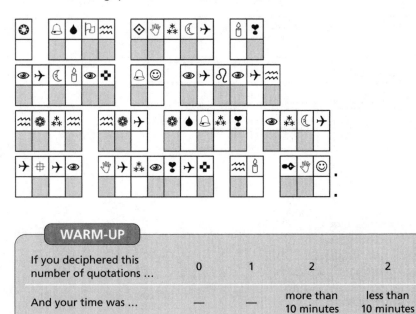

B The following quotation is from Winston Churchill.

To continue your WARM-UP, turn to page 23.

If you deciphered this number of quotations …	0	1	2	2
And your time was …	—	—	more than 10 minutes	less than 10 minutes
Neuro-points earned	0	1	2	3

WARM-UP

SOLUTIONS

A Popularity is the crown of laurel that the world puts on bad art.
B I must place on record my regret that the human race ever learned to fly.

Decipher the two quotations below. The white boxes signify vowels, and the shaded boxes signify consonants. The quotations do not use the same code. Try to decipher both quotations in 10 minutes or less.

A The following quotation is from Jane Wagner.

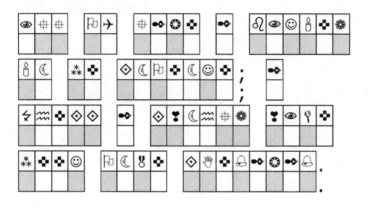

B The following quotation is from Norman Mailer.

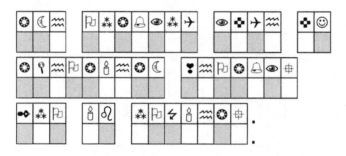

To continue your CHALLENGE, turn to page 15.

SOLUTIONS

A All my life I wanted to be someone; I guess I should have been more specific.
B The natural role of twentieth century man is anxiety.

Decipher the two quotations below. The quotations do not use the same code. Try to decipher both quotations in 10 minutes or less.

A The following quotation is from Winston Churchill.

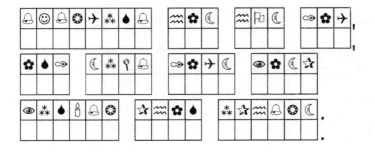

B The following quotation is from John Ruskin.

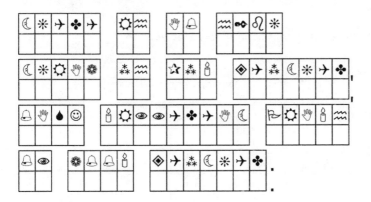

To continue your PRACTICE, turn to page 21.

SOLUTIONS

A *Everyone has his day, and some days last longer than others.*

B *There is no such thing as bad weather, only different kinds of good weather.*

Decipher the two quotations below. The quotations do not use the same code. Try to decipher both quotations in 10 minutes or less.

A *The following quotation is from Arthur Schopenhauer.*

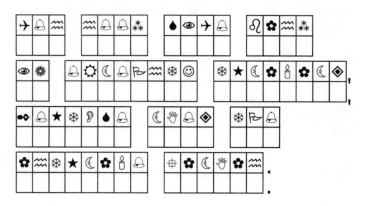

B *The following quotation is from Albert Einstein.*

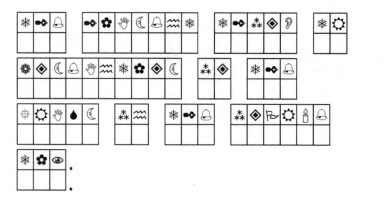

CHALLENGE

If you deciphered this number of quotations …	0	1	2	2
And your time was …	—	—	more than 10 minutes	less than 10 minutes
Neuro-points earned	0	1	2	3

To continue your CHALLENGE, turn to page 25.

SOLUTIONS

A *Men need some kind of external activity, because they are inactive within.*

B *The hardest thing to understand in the world is the income tax.*

Writing in the Stars

In this set of exercises, you will call upon your logical reasoning capacity and apply it to the field of language. A list of nine words is given, six of which can be placed in the star. To determine which of the six words are used and where each is to be placed, you must logically proceed through combinations of words according to the letter they have in common. Your working memory will guide this process, helping you develop a strategy, explore different combinations of words, and determine which words fit.

Of the nine words in each list below, only six can be placed in the star. Arrows indicate the direction in which each word is placed. To assist you, one letter has already been placed in each star. Try to fill in the two stars in five minutes or less.

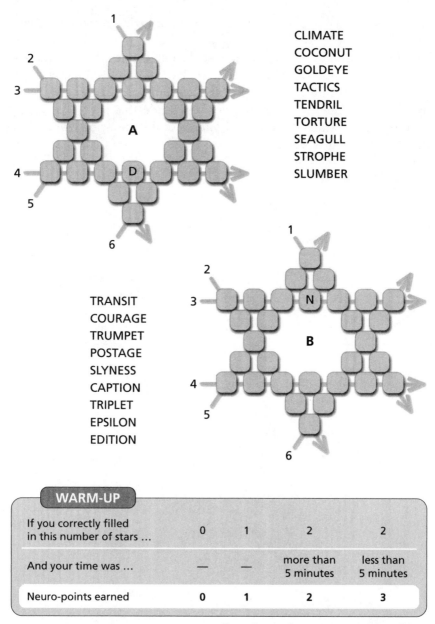

CLIMATE
COCONUT
GOLDEYE
TACTICS
TENDRIL
TORTURE
SEAGULL
STROPHE
SLUMBER

TRANSIT
COURAGE
TRUMPET
POSTAGE
SLYNESS
CAPTION
TRIPLET
EPSILON
EDITION

WARM-UP

If you correctly filled in this number of stars ...	0	1	2	2
And your time was ...	—	—	more than 5 minutes	less than 5 minutes
Neuro-points earned	0	1	2	3

To continue your WARM-UP, turn to page 32.

SOLUTIONS B 1 epsilon 2 trumpet 3 transit 4 caption 5 courage 6 triplet
A 1 seagull 2 coconut 3 climate 4 tendril 5 tactics 6 torture

Of the nine words in each list below, only six can be placed in the star. Arrows indicate the direction in which each word is placed. To assist you, one letter has already been placed in each star. Try to fill in the two stars in five minutes or less.

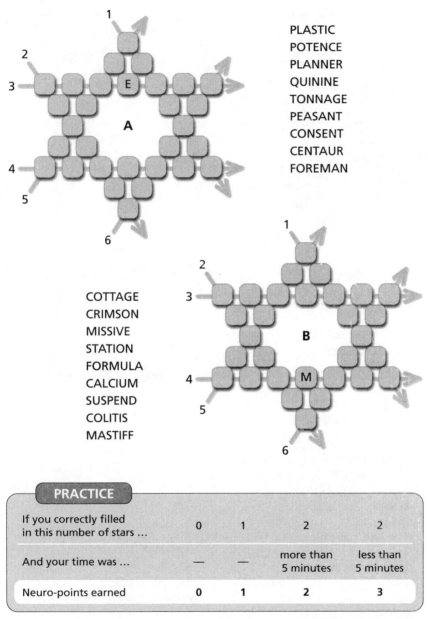

PLASTIC
POTENCE
PLANNER
QUININE
TONNAGE
PEASANT
CONSENT
CENTAUR
FOREMAN

COTTAGE
CRIMSON
MISSIVE
STATION
FORMULA
CALCIUM
SUSPEND
COLITIS
MASTIFF

To continue your PRACTICE, turn to page 28.

SOLUTIONS

A 1 centaur 2 peasant 3 potence 4 planner 5 plastic 6 tonnage
B 1 station 2 calcium 3 cottage 4 crimson 5 colitis 6 missive

Of the nine words in each list below, only six can be placed in the star. Arrows indicate the direction in which each word is placed. Try to fill in the two stars in five minutes or less.

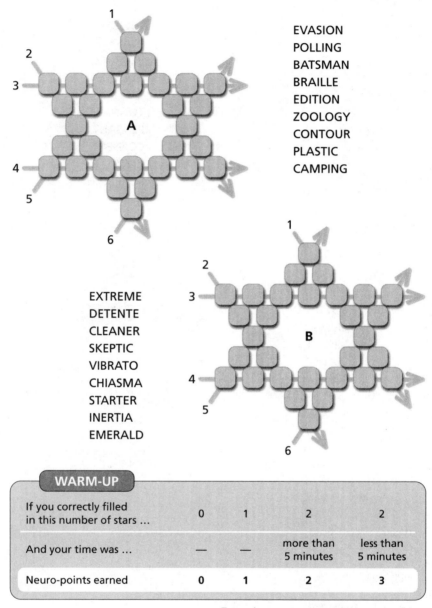

EVASION
POLLING
BATSMAN
BRAILLE
EDITION
ZOOLOGY
CONTOUR
PLASTIC
CAMPING

EXTREME
DETENTE
CLEANER
SKEPTIC
VIBRATO
CHIASMA
STARTER
INERTIA
EMERALD

WARM-UP

If you correctly filled in this number of stars ...	0	1	2	2
And your time was ...	—	—	more than 5 minutes	less than 5 minutes
Neuro-points earned	0	1	2	3

To continue your WARM-UP, turn to page 34.

SOLUTIONS *A 1 camping 2 braille 3 batsman 4 polling 5 plastic 6 edition OR 1 edition 2 plastic 3 polling 4 batsman 5 braille 6 camping B 1 cleaner 2 emerald 3 extreme 4 starter 5 skeptic 6 detente OR 1 detente 2 skeptic 3 starter 4 extreme 5 emerald 6 cleaner*

Of the nine words in each list below, only six can be placed in the star. Arrows indicate the direction in which each word is placed. Try to fill in the two stars in five minutes or less.

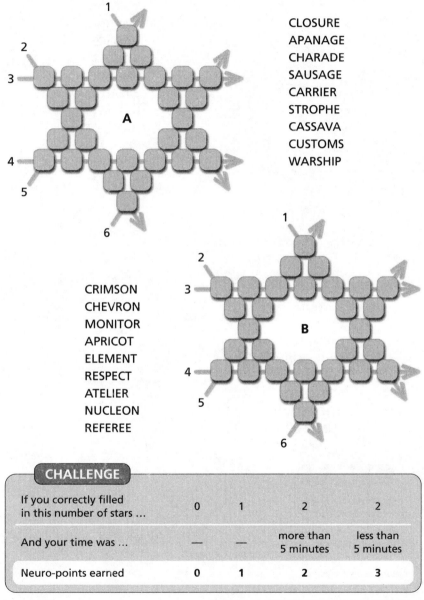

CLOSURE
APANAGE
CHARADE
SAUSAGE
CARRIER
STROPHE
CASSAVA
CUSTOMS
WARSHIP

CRIMSON
CHEVRON
MONITOR
APRICOT
ELEMENT
RESPECT
ATELIER
NUCLEON
REFEREE

CHALLENGE

If you correctly filled in this number of stars …	0	1	2	2
And your time was …	—	—	more than 5 minutes	less than 5 minutes
Neuro-points earned	0	1	2	3

To continue your CHALLENGE, turn to page 29.

SOLUTIONS A 1 sausage 2 cassava 3 closure 4 charade 5 customs 6 apanage
OR 1 apanage 2 customs 3 charade 4 closure 5 cassava 6 sausage
B 1 respect 2 chevron 3 crimson 4 apricot 5 atelier 6 nucleon
OR 1 nucleon 2 atelier 3 apricot 4 crimson 5 chevron 6 respect

Of the nine words in each list below, only six can be placed in the star. Arrows indicate the direction in which each word is placed. Try to fill in the two stars in five minutes or less.

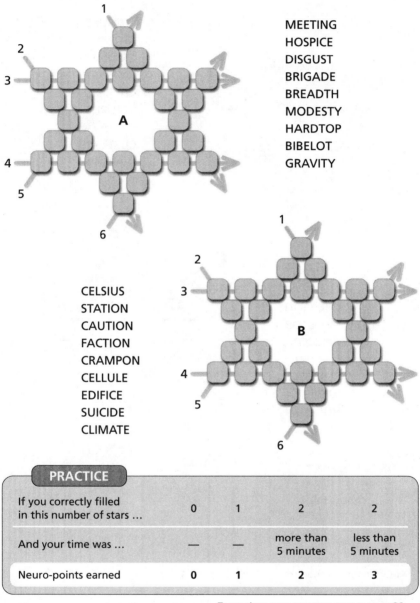

MEETING
HOSPICE
DISGUST
BRIGADE
BREADTH
MODESTY
HARDTOP
BIBELOT
GRAVITY

CELSIUS
STATION
CAUTION
FACTION
CRAMPON
CELLULE
EDIFICE
SUICIDE
CLIMATE

PRACTICE

If you correctly filled in this number of stars …	0	1	2	2
And your time was …	—	—	more than 5 minutes	less than 5 minutes
Neuro-points earned	0	1	2	3

To continue your PRACTICE, turn to page 33.

SOLUTIONS

A 1 hospice 2 meeting 3 modesty 4 brigade 5 breadth 6 gravity
OR 1 gravity 2 breadth 3 brigade 4 modesty 5 meeting 6 hospice
B 1 station 2 cellule 3 climate 4 caution 5 celsius 6 edifice
OR 1 edifice 2 celsius 3 caution 4 climate 5 cellule 6 station

Of the nine words in each list below, only six can be placed in the star. Arrows indicate the direction in which each word is placed. Try to fill in the two stars in five minutes or less.

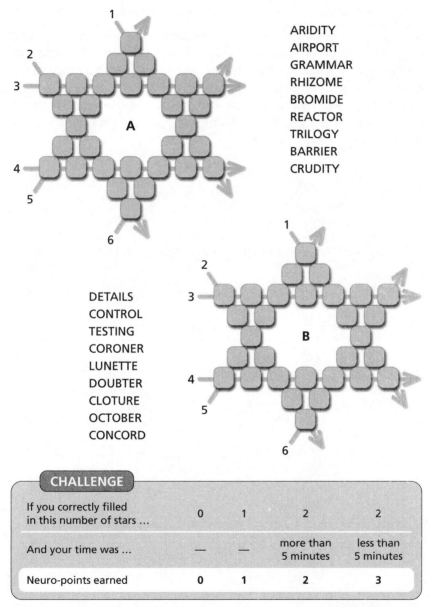

ARIDITY
AIRPORT
GRAMMAR
RHIZOME
BROMIDE
REACTOR
TRILOGY
BARRIER
CRUDITY

DETAILS
CONTROL
TESTING
CORONER
LUNETTE
DOUBTER
CLOTURE
OCTOBER
CONCORD

CHALLENGE

If you correctly filled in this number of stars ...	0	1	2	2
And your time was ...	—	—	more than 5 minutes	less than 5 minutes
Neuro-points earned	0	1	2	3

To continue your CHALLENGE, turn to page 35.

SOLUTIONS B 1 doubter 2 control 3 cloture 4 coroner 5 concord 6 lunette OR 1 lunette 2 concord 3 coroner 4 cloture 5 control 6 doubter
A 1 rhizome 2 airport 3 aridity 4 bromide 5 barrier 6 trilogy OR 1 trilogy 2 barrier 3 bromide 4 aridity 5 airport 6 rhizome

Towers of Hanoi

In this set of exercises, you are presented with five different-sized disks on three posts. Your objective is to move the disks from post to post so that they are stacked by size on a single post. You may move only one disk at a time, and you may not place a larger disk on a smaller one. To perform this exercise, you must determine the best strategy by calculating and planning the least number of moves to reach your objective.

In one minute or less, determine how many disk moves are necessary to proceed from the starting stack configuration shown in A to the target stack configuration shown in B.

A
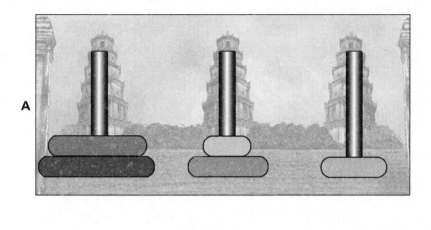

B
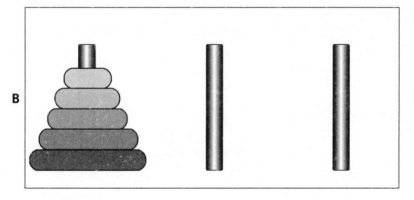

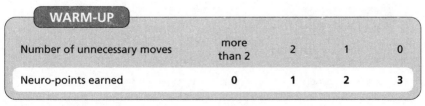

	more than 2	2	1	0
Number of unnecessary moves				
Neuro-points earned	0	1	2	3

To continue your WARM-UP, turn to page 39.

SOLUTION   *Five moves are necessary.*

In one minute or less, determine how many disk moves are necessary to proceed from the starting stack configuration shown in A to the target stack configuration shown in B.

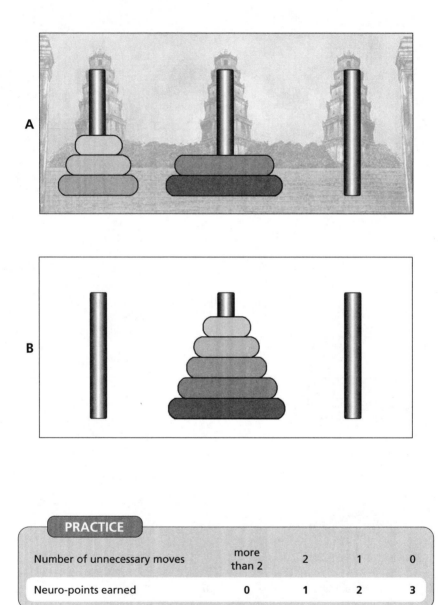

A

B

To continue your PRACTICE, turn to page 36.

PRACTICE

Number of unnecessary moves	more than 2	2	1	0
Neuro-points earned	0	1	2	3

SOLUTION   *Seven moves are necessary.*

In two minutes or less, determine how many disk moves are necessary to proceed from the starting stack configuration shown in A to the target stack configuration shown in B.

A

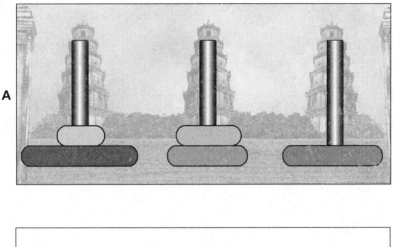

B

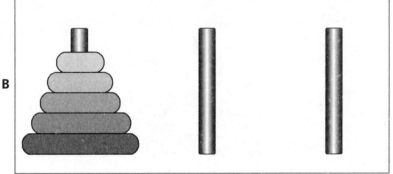

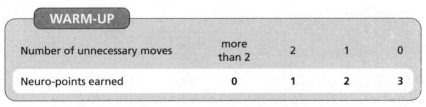

WARM-UP

Number of unnecessary moves	more than 2	2	1	0
Neuro-points earned	0	1	2	3

To continue your WARM-UP, turn to page 43.

SOLUTION   *Nine moves are necessary.*

In two minutes or less, determine how many disk moves are necessary to proceed from the starting stack configuration shown in A to the target stack configuration shown in B.

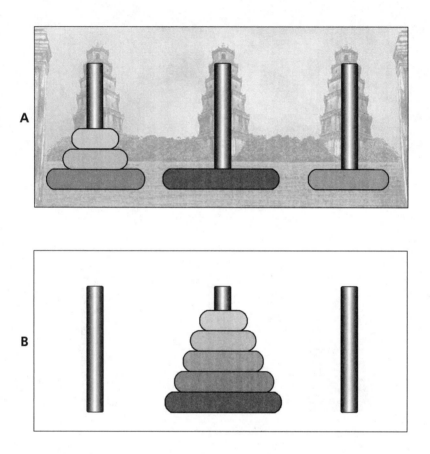

CHALLENGE

Number of unnecessary moves	more than 2	2	1	0
Neuro-points earned	0	1	2	3

To continue your CHALLENGE, turn to page 37.

SOLUTION   *Eleven moves are necessary.*

In three minutes or less, determine how many disk moves are necessary to proceed from the starting stack configuration shown in A to the target stack configuration shown in B.

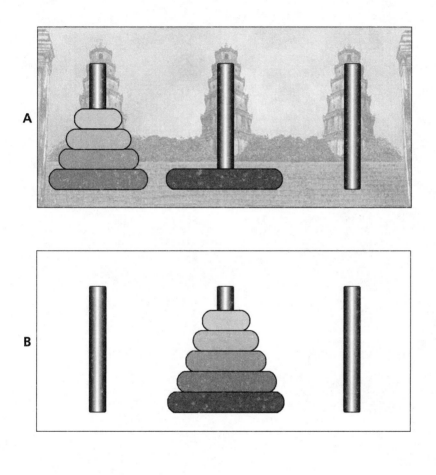

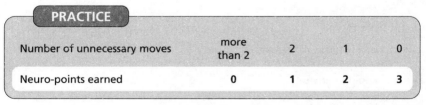

To continue your PRACTICE, turn to page 41.

SOLUTION Fifteen moves are necessary.

In three minutes or less, determine how many disk moves are necessary to proceed from the starting stack configuration shown in A to the target stack configuration shown in B.

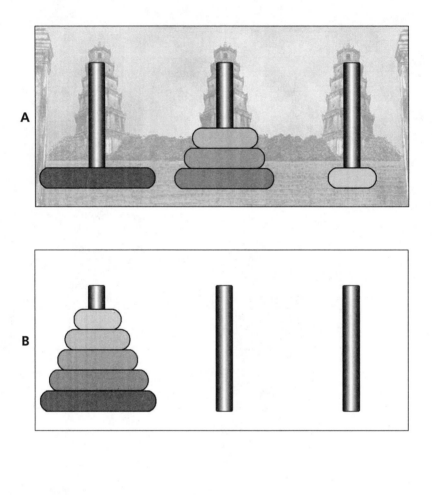

To continue your CHALLENGE, turn to page 45.

CHALLENGE

Number of unnecessary moves	more than 2	2	1	0
Neuro-points earned	0	1	2	3

SOLUTION   *Fourteen moves are necessary.*

Hurray for Change

This set of exercises requires strategic and flexible thinking. You will need to alternate between two parallel ways of thinking—whether between two alphabetical systems or between an alphabetical progression and a numerical progression. Since the elements are dispersed on the page, you will also need to call upon your visual and spatial skills.

In the example below, the objective is to alternately link furniture-related words and family-related words, maintaining alphabetical order in each of the two groups of words.

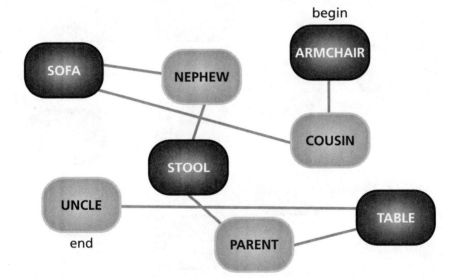

You begin with *armchair* (the first furniture-related word), link it to *cousin* (the family-related word that is first in alphabetical order), then *sofa,* and so on, until you arrive at *uncle.*

*The seven light lozenges below contain words, and the seven dark lozenges contain numbers. In one minute or less, begin at **card** and alternately link word and number lozenges in ascending order until you arrive at **1976**. Once you begin, you may not modify a link or use the same lozenge twice.*

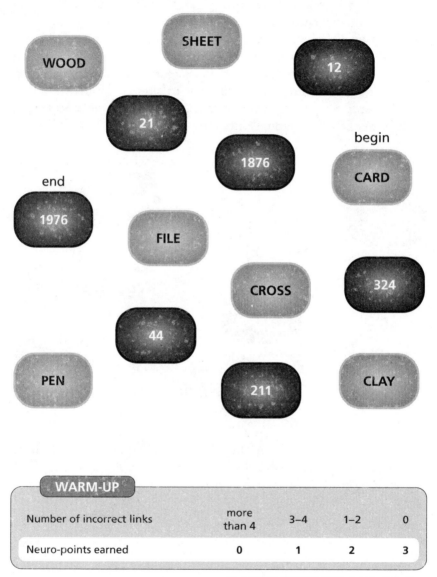

WARM-UP				
Number of incorrect links	more than 4	3–4	1–2	0
Neuro-points earned	0	1	2	3

To continue your WARM-UP, turn to page 9.

SOLUTION   card, 12, clay, 21, cross, 44, file, 211, pen, 324, sheet, 1876, wood, 1976

The seven dark lozenges below contain words, and the seven light lozenges contain numbers. In one minute or less, begin at **aisle** and alternately link word and number lozenges in ascending order until you arrive at **7812**. Once you begin, you may not modify a link or use the same lozenge twice.

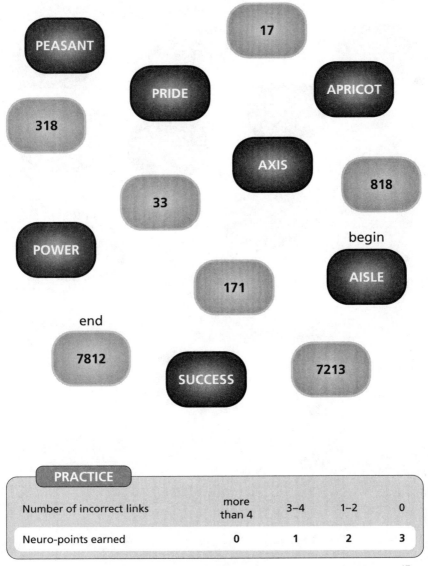

PEASANT

17

PRIDE

APRICOT

318

AXIS

818

33

begin

POWER

AISLE

171

end

7812

SUCCESS

7213

PRACTICE				
Number of incorrect links	more than 4	3–4	1–2	0
Neuro-points earned	0	1	2	3

To continue your PRACTICE, turn to page 47.

SOLUTION aisle, 17, apricot, 33, axis, 171, peasant, 318, power, 818, pride, 7213, success, 7812

The seven dark lozenges below contain words, and the seven light lozenges contain numbers. In one minute or less, begin at **1257** and alternately link number and word lozenges in ascending order until you arrive at **western**. Once you begin, you may not modify a link or use the same lozenge twice.

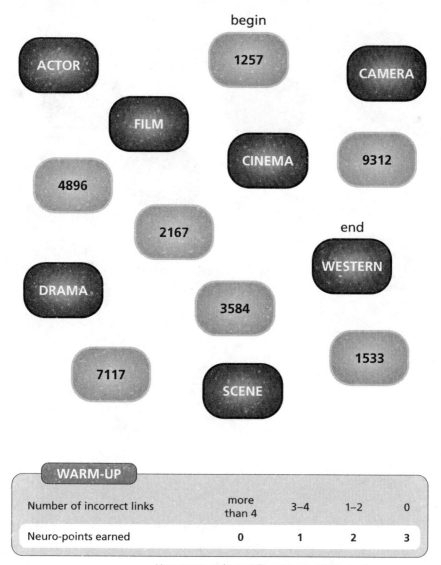

Number of incorrect links	more than 4	3–4	1–2	0
Neuro-points earned	0	1	2	3

WARM-UP

Your WARM-UP is over! Turn to page 204 to total your score.
Then turn to page 7 to begin your PRACTICE.

SOLUTION   1257, actor, 1533, camera, 2167, cinema, 3584, drama, 4896, film, 7117, scene, 9312, western

The seven light lozenges below contain words, and the seven dark lozenges contain numbers. In one minute or less, begin at **hill** and alternately link word and number lozenges in ascending order until you arrive at **9312**. Once you begin, you may not modify a link or use the same lozenge twice.

CHALLENGE

Number of incorrect links	more than 4	3–4	1–2	0
Neuro-points earned	0	1	2	3

To continue your CHALLENGE, turn to page 49.

SOLUTION hill, 1954, mountain, 1975, peak, 3914, plain, 4368, ridge, 5029, summit, 7217, valley, 9312

Both sets of seven light and dark lozenges below contain words.
In one minute or less, begin at **acrobat** and alternately link light and
dark lozenges in ascending alphabetical order until you arrive at **typhoon**.
Once you begin, you may not modify a link or use the same lozenge
twice.

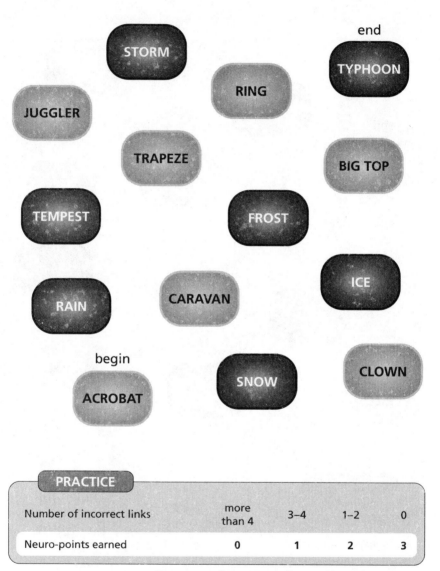

end

STORM

RING

TYPHOON

JUGGLER

TRAPEZE

BIG TOP

TEMPEST

FROST

ICE

RAIN

CARAVAN

begin

CLOWN

SNOW

ACROBAT

PRACTICE

Number of incorrect links	more than 4	3–4	1–2	0
Neuro-points earned	0	1	2	3

Your PRACTICE is over! Turn to page 206 to total your score.
Then turn to page 11 to begin your CHALLENGE.

SOLUTION   acrobat, frost, big top, ice, caravan, rain, clown, snow,
juggler, storm, ring, tempest, trapeze, typhoon

Both sets of seven light and dark lozenges below contain words. In one minute or less, begin at **comet** and alternately link dark and light lozenges in ascending alphabetical order until you arrive at **tennis**. Once you begin, you may not modify a link or use the same lozenge twice.

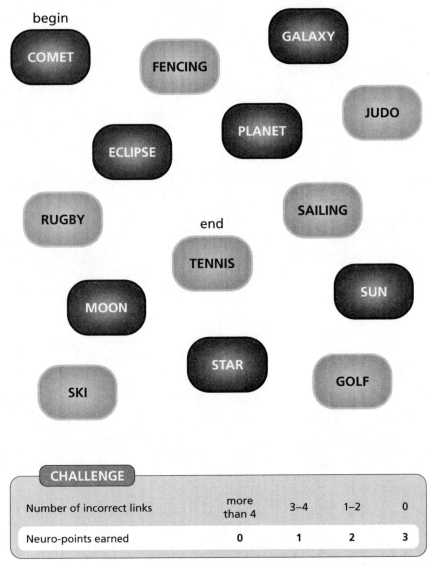

begin

COMET

FENCING

GALAXY

JUDO

PLANET

ECLIPSE

RUGBY

SAILING

end

TENNIS

MOON

SUN

STAR

GOLF

SKI

CHALLENGE

Number of incorrect links	more than 4	3–4	1–2	0
Neuro-points earned	0	1	2	3

Your CHALLENGE is over! Turn to page 208 to total your score.

SOLUTION comet, fencing, eclipse, golf, galaxy, judo, moon, rugby, planet, sailing, star, ski, sun, tennis

SCORING RESULTS

Scoring Chart for WARM-UP Exercises

Circle the number of neuro-points you earned for each exercise.
After completing all the exercises, total your scores.

PAGE	NUMBER OF POINTS			
6	0	1	2	3
56	0	1	2	3
107	0	1	2	3
141	0	1	2	3
175	0	1	2	3
20	0	1	2	3
70	0	1	2	3
116	0	1	2	3
150	0	1	2	3
182	0	1	2	3
32	0	1	2	3
84	0	1	2	3
123	0	1	2	3
157	0	1	2	3
189	0	1	2	3
40	0	1	2	3
96	0	1	2	3
130	0	1	2	3
164	0	1	2	3
196	0	1	2	3
10	0	1	2	3
60	0	1	2	3
109	0	1	2	3
143	0	1	2	3
177	0	1	2	3
24	0	1	2	3
74	0	1	2	3
118	0	1	2	3
152	0	1	2	3
184	0	1	2	3
34	0	1	2	3
88	0	1	2	3
125	0	1	2	3
159	0	1	2	3
191	0	1	2	3
44	0	1	2	3
98	0	1	2	3
132	0	1	2	3
166	0	1	2	3
198	0	1	2	3

Number of circles in each column

×1   ×2   ×3

TOTAL   +   +   =   NEURO-POINTS

If you earned 0 to 40 neuro-points ...

> Perhaps you haven't been practicing your cognitive skills often
> enough, or perhaps you're just getting started. The good news is,
> there are plenty of exercises in this book that you can use to
> improve!

If you earned 41 to 80 neuro-points ...

> This is only the warm-up, and it's clear that your brain is eager
> to work more. Now that you are familiar with the principles of the
> exercises, you have everything you need to succeed. Get pumped
> up and try again.

If you earned 81 to 120 neuro-points ...

> Excellent results! You aren't the type of person whose brain dozes
> off. Whether you're reading, playing intellectually stimulating games,
> or doing crossword puzzles, you know what a mental workout is.
> Don't let this go to your head, however; there are many challenges
> that await you, and some of them will definitely put your brain
> to the test.

Scoring Chart for PRACTICE Exercises

Circle the number of neuro-points you earned for each exercise.
After completing all the exercises, total your scores.

PAGE	NUMBER OF POINTS			
8	0	1	2	3
64	0	1	2	3
108	0	1	2	3
146	0	1	2	3
176	0	1	2	3
14	0	1	2	3
58	0	1	2	3
112	0	1	2	3
142	0	1	2	3
179	0	1	2	3
22	0	1	2	3
78	0	1	2	3
117	0	1	2	3
154	0	1	2	3
183	0	1	2	3
28	0	1	2	3
72	0	1	2	3
120	0	1	2	3
151	0	1	2	3
186	0	1	2	3
33	0	1	2	3
92	0	1	2	3
124	0	1	2	3
161	0	1	2	3
190	0	1	2	3
36	0	1	2	3
86	0	1	2	3
127	0	1	2	3
158	0	1	2	3
193	0	1	2	3
42	0	1	2	3
100	0	1	2	3
131	0	1	2	3
168	0	1	2	3
197	0	1	2	3
48	0	1	2	3
97	0	1	2	3
134	0	1	2	3
165	0	1	2	3
200	0	1	2	3

Number of circles in each column

$\times 1$　$\times 2$　$\times 3$

TOTAL　　　＿＿＿ ＋ ＿＿＿ ＋ ＿＿＿ ＝ ＿＿＿ NEURO-POINTS

If you earned 0 to 40 neuro-points ...

You're working hard, but your mind is still becoming familiar with the cognitive skills needed to win at these exercises. Don't lose heart—as they say, practice makes perfect!

If you earned 41 to 80 neuro-points ...

You're beginning to understand the principles of these exercises. Your results are encouraging and prove that you have great cognitive abilities. Carry on—you can only get better!

If you earned 81 to 120 neuro-points ...

You obviously have the makings of a brain master. You excel at the techniques required by these exercises. Try to achieve even better scores at the CHALLENGE level!

Scoring Chart for CHALLENGE Exercises

*Circle the number of neuro-points you earned for each exercise.
After completing all the exercises, total your scores.*

PAGE	NUMBER OF POINTS			
12	0	1	2	3
66	0	1	2	3
110	0	1	2	3
148	0	1	2	3
178	0	1	2	3
16	0	1	2	3
62	0	1	2	3
114	0	1	2	3
144	0	1	2	3
180	0	1	2	3
26	0	1	2	3
80	0	1	2	3
119	0	1	2	3
155	0	1	2	3
185	0	1	2	3
30	0	1	2	3
76	0	1	2	3
121	0	1	2	3
153	0	1	2	3
187	0	1	2	3
35	0	1	2	3
94	0	1	2	3
126	0	1	2	3
162	0	1	2	3
192	0	1	2	3
37	0	1	2	3
90	0	1	2	3
128	0	1	2	3
160	0	1	2	3
194	0	1	2	3
46	0	1	2	3
101	0	1	2	3
133	0	1	2	3
169	0	1	2	3
199	0	1	2	3
50	0	1	2	3
99	0	1	2	3
135	0	1	2	3
167	0	1	2	3
201	0	1	2	3

Number of circles in each column

×1   ×2   ×3

TOTAL   ___ + ___ + ___ = ___ NEURO-POINTS

If you earned 0 to 40 neuro-points ...

If your results aren't as good as you expected, perhaps the CHALLENGE level was too intense for you at this point. Don't worry— hit the mind gym again, and remember: No pain, no gain!

If you earned 41 to 80 neuro-points ...

Good job! You have managed to call upon your cognitive skills to pass a number of challenges. Perhaps you need to work on your speed in order to achieve top results.

If you earned 81 to 120 neuro-points ...

Congratulations! Your results are excellent! Your neurons are in great shape, and thanks to your cognitive skills and speed, you have managed to reach the highest level of these challenging exercises. Continue to seek out new challenges to keep your brain healthy and active.

ABOUT THE AUTHORS

Michel Noir, Ph.D., holds advanced degrees in cognitive psychology and education and is a cofounder and the C.E.O. of Scientific Brain Training (www.happyneuron.com), a company dedicated to educating the public about brain health and providing a line of mental fitness products.

Bernard Croisile, M.D., Ph.D., is a leading neurologist and an expert on the aging brain. He has written 100 peer-reviewed articles and spoken at numerous conferences on the brain and Alzheimer's disease. In addition, he is a cofounder and the Vice President–Scientific at Scientific Brain Training (www.happyneuron.com).